Slavery Books & African American History Resources
https://slaverybooks.blogspot.com

Prepared for Publication
By
HISTORIC PUBLISHING
San Antonio, Texas
©2017
All Rights Reserved
HISTORIC PUBLISHING

Slavery Books & African American History Resources
https://slaverybooks.blogspot.com /

IDLE COMMENTS

IDLE COMMENTS

BY

ISAAC ERWIN AVERY
Late City Editor of the Charlotte Observer

CHARLOTTE, N. C.
THE AVERY PUBLISHING COMPANY
1905

Copyright, 1905
By GEORGE STEPHENS
Publishers' Printing Company
New York

PREFACE

IMMEDIATELY after Mr. Avery's untimely and tragic death, there was a demand throughout the State that there should be published a memorial volume consisting of selections from his writings. Mr. D. A. Tompkins, Mr. George Stephens, W. H. Twitty and Mr. Chase Brenizer, all of Charlotte, appreciating the importance of the suggestion, assumed the financial responsibility of such a volume. In addition, they conceived the idea that, by the sale of the book, memorial scholarships might be established at Trinity College, Mr. Avery's alma mater. They asked the undersigned board of editors to prepare the volume.

The editors now present what is, in their judgment, the best work of this gifted man. We have endeavored to make the selections of such a varied interest as to show at once the versatility of his mind and to appeal to all classes of readers. There has been no revision of his work--with a very few unimportant changes the selections are just as he wrote them. There is no better evidence of his genius than the fact that writing, done at times with such great haste and with the pressure of night work upon him, should be so strikingly free from infelicities of diction.

It is the opinion of the editors that the present volume is evidence at once of Mr. Avery's literary ability, and a record of life in North Carolina such as has not been published in the State. We believe, too, that he treated local affairs and local characters with such an unerring knowledge of human nature that his writings will appeal to men of other sections. We bespeak for the volume of a hearty reception by those who knew him in the flesh and felt the charm of his personality; by those who never saw him, but followed his words as eagerly as those of an intimate friend and a genial philosopher; by those who, not having known him before may find here the revelation of a very rare spirit.

EDWIN MIMS,
J. P. CALDWELL,
C. ALPHONSO SMITH,
PLATO DURHAM,
J. W. BAILEY.

ISAAC ERWIN AVERY

ISAAC ERWIN AVERY was born at the ancestral home of the Averys, at Swan Ponds, about four miles from Morganton, in Burke county, N. C., on the first day of December, 1871, and died at Charlotte, on the second day of April, 1904. He was the second son of Hon. Alphonso C. Avery and Susan Morrison Avery, and was descended from families whose members were prominent in the country's history. His parents moved to Morganton when he was very young, and there his boyhood days were spent, attending the primary schools. He was prepared for college at the Academy of Morganton by Rev. John A. Gilmer, now the Presbyterian minister at Newton, N. C., and might have entered college at the age of sixteen, but remained at home for a while, devoting most of his time to reading. His fondness for reading developed when a mere boy, as did his propensity for writing humorous letters and compositions. He spent some months in the service of the Western North Carolina Railroad Company, at Morganton and Hot Springs. For six months or more prior to entering college he served as collector for the Bank of Morganton. He entered the sophomore class of Trinity College (then located in Randolph county, and later moved to Durham) in 1890, and his course there was marked by a special fondness for history and literature. He was an excellent football player, and was universally esteemed by faculty and students. During his senior year he read law under his father, the dean of the law department of Trinity, and when licensed, in September, 1893, was, to say the least, as well prepared as any candidate in the large class which went before the Supreme Court.

While he was regarded by all who came in contact with him as possessing a mind especially fitted for the law, his tastes and talents were constantly driving him toward newspaper and more general literary work. He had made good progress along this line before leaving college, as editor of The Trinity Archive and as correspondent for different papers in the State. His first contribution which earned him money was a paragraph of about thirty lines sent to Town Topics, without hope of reward, during the Christmas vacation of 1892. For this he received ten dollars. This incident led to dreams of making reputation and support some day as a writer.

Soon after receiving his license to practice law, Mr. Avery returned to Morganton and was employed by Mr. W. C. Erwin as associate editor of The Morganton Herald. Here he exercised a free hand in writing for the paper, and attracted considerable outside attention by his original methods and the excellent humor in many of his articles. Upon the invitation of Mr. Thomas P. Jernigan, then a citizen of Raleigh, who had been appointed by President Cleveland consul-general at Shanghai, Mr. Avery left for China in March, 1894, as secretary to the consul-general. In less than a year he was appointed vice consul-general at Shanghai, which office he filled until the spring of 1898, when a new consul-general was named by President McKinley. In China Mr. Avery did some writing for American newspapers, but decided not to continue the work, owing to his connection with the consular service. He was, however, during a large part of his stay in Shanghai a regular contributor to The North China Daily News, the leading English paper in the Orient. While residing in Shanghai, Mr. Avery was prominent in the leading social circle among the foreign residents and absorbed a rich fund of information which stood him in good stead later, and made him a most interesting talker not only about things in the Far East, but in the world at large.

When he returned to North Carolina, he took up active newspaper work after a few months, reporting the proceedings of the State Senate in the Legislature of 1899 for a number of newspapers represented by Col. Fred A. Olds, of Raleigh. He also had charge of Colonel Old's news bureau for a month or more while he was on a trip to Cuba. About May 1, 1899, he went to Greensboro, where he established a news bureau, representing a number of leading papers in North Carolina and elsewhere. As a result of his activity as a reporter, Greensboro became especially prominent as a news-dispensing centre, and Mr. Avery's reputation as a writer began to expand. On January 1, 1900, he became city editor of the Charlotte Observer, which position he filled until his death. It was while here that his unusual literary gifts to some extent gained the recognition which they really deserved.

Personally he was the most engaging of men. Handsome as Apollo, with a countenance clear-cut and proclaiming in every line his gentle birth; tall, massive of frame, he combined with these physical attributes a manner as genial as the sunshine. His cultivation was that of the schools, that acquired by the reading of the best literature and of close association with, and acute observation of, the great world of men. His gifts of conversation were equal to those with which he had been endowed for his profession, and thus he was with these, and his commanding presence, the centre of every group in which he found himself. His popularity was unbounded. In his great heart was charity for all mankind, and it was ever open to the cry of distress. None who knew him or followed him in his work will ever forget him or cease to mourn that his life, so rich in promise, should have been cut off before its sun had nearly reached meridian.

During his four years' sojourn in Charlotte Mr. Avery became thoroughly identified with the best phases of the city's life, and was a recognized leader in almost every movement that promised benefit to the people. While he was a leader in the best social life of the city, he was popular with all classes. He was especially sought after by those in trouble, whether friends or strangers, and though his time was generally taken up to a large extent with his newspaper work and calls made upon him by society, he always took that necessary to offer counsel to those who called on him. Though exceedingly patient and genuinely anxious to aid all who appealed to him, he would, on rare occasions, remark with a sigh that he wished he did not know of so much unhappiness--had not been made to put himself in the places of so many people in distress. But this feeling was only momentary, for he would immediately turn his thoughts to other things and become again the possessor of that sunny disposition which was one of his most charming characteristics.

While Mr. Avery was designated as "city editor" of the Charlotte Observer, he was in reality much more, for he was given freedom to criticise or commend the public acts of men which came under his observation, and while he never failed to write what he thought, he did it in a way that made him few enemies, even among those whose actions suffered most at his hand. While he was most widely known because of his manner of handling stories of human interest, either pathetic or humorous, as a miscellaneous news-gatherer he was eminently successful, thus combining gifts rarely developed in the same nature. So famous did his writing become that it was not unusual for papers published hundreds of miles from Charlotte to reprint his reports of events which, written in the ordinary manner, would interest none save those residing in the immediate vicinity in which the incidents detailed occurred. Another rather unusual combination noticeable in his newspaper work was his ability to write pathetic as well as humorous articles. He could do either with equal readiness, yet his natural propensity was toward that of humor--the clean, sweet and yet sharp and sparkling kind that would cause a laugh, and do more. In his general newspaper work, where he was confined to no special class of events, but had the entire field at his disposal, he seemed never at a loss as to how a story should be written, and he made remarkably few mistakes. This statement is, of course, intended to convey the idea that Mr. Avery was a student of human nature. In fact, he seemed to know men at first sight, and his ability to pick out a fraudulent scheme when first unfolded to him--no matter how well clothed--was noticeable on many occasions, and the value of this clear-sightedness in his work as city editor was incalculable.

Mr. Avery could not only gather the news which was on the surface, so to speak, and put it in the proper shape to go before an intelligent public, but he could readily induce people to give out particulars that are legitimate matters of publicity, but which are often withheld by those who possess the information desired. Therefore, he was preëminently known among his newspaper associates as the best of interviewers. Whenever an occurrence of special importance came to light, no matter where, the first thought in the Observer office was that Avery should be on the ground, and whenever it was possible to do so, he was sent at once to the scene. Who can ever forget his stories of the mill disaster in South Carolina? or his account of the Greensboro reunion? His paper received numerous requests to have him assigned to out-of-town meetings and other events which it was desired should be handled in a masterly manner.

In exercising the prerogatives of his position, it often fell to his lot to pass unfavorable criticism upon men or systems. He did this in such manner as he thought appropriate, and now and then a controversy would develop, but he invariably contented himself with merely stating his position clearly, being satisfied to let the public draw its own conclusions. On a few occasions his humorous references to people brought them to see him, to protest that they should not have been referred to in the manner which he had seen fit to employ. Here, too, he was especially gifted, for without any semblance of a compromise, he would make peace in a way that would sometimes provoke envy in his newspaper associates, and in rare instances disappoint them when they thought he might have to essay the role to which by nature he seemed especially fitted in a physical sense, owing to the bellicose vein into which the aggrieved party had brought himself on reading Mr. Avery's description of him.

More significant than his work as a reporter or an interviewer or an editorial writer was his "A Variety of Idle Comment,"--a department of the

Observer which appeared on Monday mornings--and upon this department his fame largely rests. A man of the world, of contact with all sorts and conditions of humanity, he had closely studied his fellows and looked "quite through the deeds of men." A commentator upon their virtues and vices, their merits and weaknesses, he brought to every discussion the subtlest analysis, and with perfect, sometimes startling, fidelity, "held the mirror up to nature." His pen was adapted with utmost facility to every subject he touched, and he touched none but to adorn or illumine it. Amiable, sweet of spirit, he yet might feel that a person, a custom or an institution called for invective or ridicule, and he was a torrent. Anon a child, a flower, a friendless one appealed to him, and his pen caressed them, as his heart was attuned to the music of the spheres. His humor was exquisite; his pathos tear-compelling. He was the master of a rich vocabulary--the master; that is the word. It responded immediately to every demand upon it, and thus he attempted no figure that was not complete; he drew no picture that did not stand out on the canvas in colors of living light. The writer professes some familiarity with the contemporaneous newspaper writers of the South, and is sure that he indulges no exuberance of language, that personal affection warps his judgment not at all, when he says that for original thought, for power or felicity of expression, Isaac Erwin Avery had not an equal among them.

CONTENTS.

- CHAPTER
  I. IN AND ABOUT A NEWSPAPER OFFICE 15
- II. CHARLOTTE AND HER NEIGHBORS 28
- III. CHARACTER SKETCHES 45
- IV. NEGRO TYPES 64
- V. WOMAN AND HER WORLD 74
- VI. CHILDREN 94
- VII. ANIMALS . . . . .
- VIII. CHRISTMAS 106
- IX. SOUTHERN LIFE AND MANNERS . . . . .
- X. ANECDOTES . . . . .
- XI. OBSERVATIONS ON LITERATURE . . . . .
- XII. IDEALS OF WRITING AND SPEAKING . . . . .
- XIII. MUSIC AND DRAMA . . . . .
- XIV. REFLECTIONS ON LIFE AND DEATH . . . . .
- XV. MISCELLANY . . . . .

THE violets again--little wet violets, and there is the clean, sweet breath of spring. One would lift his head and drink deep--taste this newness, this grateful freshness that is about. There is a quicker leap of life, and Nature seems to stir with a kind of tenderness. There is deeper glow on the faces of children--easier happiness on a tiny, nestling face. . . . Girlhood comes to outward whiteness again--the cool, crisp sign of spring. And in all is the subtle charm of violets--little human, tremulous things, gentle as love's whisper, pure as purity. Restful, quaint little flower, too--simple, appealing. . . . Flower to lay on a baby that has died--to give as seemly tribute to womanhood--to press against the face as easement for tired heart. . . . Such a dear, peaceful little flower, all alone in flower-land--emblems of the world's simplest and best, and waiting to mock a false face or adorn the beauty that comes from the soul.

IDLE COMMENTS

CHAPTER I
IN AND ABOUT A NEWSPAPER OFFICE

How the News Was Sent

THE public is probably now able to understand the strain that has been upon newspapers in recent days. The burden of a great crisis has rested severely upon the daily press. Its members, part of the machine, have had personal feeling, also, but everything with them had to be subordinated to the ever-pressing task of conveying correct intelligence to the world.

Blessed with favorable service, The Observer was one of the only two papers in the State that sent out from their own towns early yesterday morning the news of the President's death. The statement is made not boastfully; for the mere purpose of this writing is to explain what the fateful news meant to a morning paper in Charlotte, far removed from the more densely populated centres.

The sending of the news and the manner of the sending was not a little thing, and there is pardonable pride in this saying. Early in the night the despatches had showed that the end was to be expected at any time, and in preparation for the sad certainty, all matter outside of press service was ordered to be rushed, and was rushed.

There was but little talk in the print shop. Every man waited--and waited.

At 2 o'clock the forms from which the paper is printed were scattered lead and iron. A fateful wire was to decide the exact mode of their arrangement and until it came there could be but indecision. And the time for carrying those forms to the press room, in some shape, was drawing nigh.

At 2:17 o'clock the paper's Associated Press operator received the wire announcing the death of the President.

* President McKinley

The message came out to the composing room, and a dozen and more men breathed a prayer for time.

The mailing clerk had received orders that would require The Observer to issue the largest edition ever sent out. The staff and the mechanical force knew that the paper, to make the mails, must go to press an hour earlier than usual, and this demanded all that mind and quickness could do.

System won out. Every man kept down nerves and worked for what he knew he must do and do quickly. The minutes passed--and the press downstairs waited.

And the paper won out. In just exactly an hour after the telegram was received the forms were in the press. No mail was missed, and, at every point that The Observer reached, its distribution was unprecedented in its history.

The Night Gang

To-day Mr. Howard A. Banks will cease to be managing editor of The Observer and will become editor of The Evening Chronicle. For eleven years he has done most of his work at night and his best work after midnight; but now he is privileged to eat breakfast and labor with a work-a-day world. He will join the throng that becomes drowsy at noon and shakes its head when it looks at the toilers of the night. Mr. Banks is to be a white man indeed, and he welcomes the change--doubtfully. He must learn to become a-weary at an hour that seems too soon--must learn to sleep too quickly. He must overcome the habits of the long years. He will do this, for man is an adaptable animal and yields easily to change. But, mayhap, he will not live so long that he can forget the charm that was while a world slumbered. He has been part of a coatless crowd that loitered on the deserted streets and feasted and lied cheerily every morning just before daylight. 'Twas such a little crowd. Month after month and year after year there were the same men who touched elbows, felt a common excitement, got closer together--found intense existence in the great stillness. Aye, Banks will be a white man, but he will not forget. Night work eats into the brain and body. 'Tis fascinating. There is charm in the late, quiet hours, in the view of a resting city, in the fine, loud silence of the night. Peace broods, and here is a time for thought. Night! Ah, night breaks too often into day. It is the blessed boon that comes after the fretfulness and bother that one sees under sunlight. It is too precious for sleep; and it is sweetest and purest after midnight. But Banks will try to forget this. He has broken the ranks and shed his raiment of Bohemianism. He, as good a comrade as ever watched the sun rise, may learn to pity the children of the night, though he knows they wish for no pity. He is the first deserter--the first to become civilized, and his going seems almost as if someone or something had died. There is no one who has a readier sympathy than Banks--no one who has such a profound appreciation of pie at 4 o'clock in the morning.

The Red-headed Foreman

It is strange to note the contrasting elements in one mere man. Look at Dick Allen, the red-headed foreman up stairs. Whenever he wants to give himself a treat he sends over to the restaurant and buys a pickled pig's foot and a cream puff. He must always have the two things together and at once. They appeal to both sides of his nature. The pig's foot soothes the part of him that chews tobacco and swears at the devil; while his love for cream puffs is akin to the thing in him that sets him to roaming, as a disciple of Izaak Walton, by the side of little rivers. The foreman is a contradiction and knows it. He is the sort of a man who likes both garlic and silk suspenders. Mr. Howard A. Banks, of the paper, has a fashion of throwing open his window at eventide in order that he may be fully bathed in the glories of the dying sun. "And I want to say, Mr. Banks," said the foreman, "that since you have been looking so much at these sunsets I am working me up a taste for the things myself." That was a cream puff mood--the foreman at his highest sentimental ebb; and yet even then he would have been far more appreciative of the sunset if he had held a stout pig's foot in his right hand. Such is the composition of Dick Allen, foreman.

The Newsboy

In the biographies of some of the modern big men the statement is frequently made that "he began life as a newsboy," the suggestion being that the man not only commenced at the bottom rung of the ladder, but that he surprised everybody by his rise from such an humble calling. The truth is that the lad who sticks to the work of carrying papers for a morning newspaper shows grit enough to accomplish anything. Every morning the carriers troop in here about 4 o'clock with sleep still heavy in their eyes. Summer and winter it is the same; they never fail; and yet they are little bits of chaps between 10 and 14 years of age. It is no small thing, and it is more than a man's work, to leave a comfortable bed before daybreak and go out into the darkness, and toil. The newsboy is a most reliable employee, and the thing in him that keeps him at his arduous task generally makes him a successful man in the long run. The young men in Charlotte and elsewhere who have been newsboys have done well in business life. They had pluck to begin with, and their training as paper carriers equipped them with the right sort of stuff for a struggle.

There is a little bit of a chap who gets up early in the morning and sells this paper, and he is around again in the afternoon to sell The Chronicle. He is a serious-eyed boy who doesn't seem to enjoy life very much, but he is a hard worker and makes a good deal of money out of the sales of his papers. He is devoted to his mother and wishes to take her every cent he makes, and he does this except when his father gets his money and spends it for drink. He cuffed the child on the streets a few days ago, led him home and emptied his pockets, and forced him to appear here next morning, shamefaced because he couldn't make a settlement for his papers and was too loyal to tell what had happened. This sort of treatment is almost an every-day occurrence, and it might as well be stopped. There is no law to act in the matter, but the next time the father mistreats that child or steals money from him to spend in drink, the writer, who will learn the truth, is going to print the name of the father and indulge in the nauseating task of dissecting him as a species of vampire parent. The father will read this and will understand exactly what is meant. He can very easily go to work and let that boy alone. Otherwise he will be exposed to the public for being the sort of brute that he really is.

Mr. Frank Johnston, 12 years old, seller of newspapers and denizen of The Observer press room, goes over to the restaurant and quarrels if his poached eggs are not cooked to his notion. He throws down a dollar in payment and carelessly jams the change into his pocket. And the man who watched him found a thing that was wrong. Mr. Johnston has grown old too quickly. He has learned the sweetness of independence, but he is missing the rarest joy of living. For now there is no one to give Mr. Johnston a quarter, and a quarter would not quicken his pulse one beat if 'twere given him. Despite his tender years, he can never have the most hallowed experience of childhood. To be given a quarter on a Saturday, say! To feel the keen little thrill in the blood; to trot down the walkway--trying not to run--to face the open street and the stores with a whole quarter in one's pocket! Man, do you remember? And have you ever been satisfied with any amount of money that you had except just that childhood's quarter? It meant mental revelry, the great, beautiful gloat--the sureness of purchasing the coveted things in the world. It meant transcendent cause for envy--an admitted superiority over all the other little boys who hadn't quarters. A quarter marked the chiefest epoch in life; it showed you to be a bit of a king with a chattering troop in your train--unquartered subjects who gazed on you admiringly, wistfully. Your small heart well nigh burst with exultation--surging so in its fresh pæan of bliss.

Ah, you lose, Mr. Johnston. God bless you, Mr. Johnston, you have lost.

The Devil and the Eel

Never was such an eel as the devil caught the other night. The red-headed foreman, who is an authority on such matters, said so, and the fat boy who attends to the engine down in the basement swore that he had caught eels from Town Creek to the Catawba and he had never seen such a fine fish. The incident marked an epoch in the life of the devil. His name is Van something; he is any age under sixteen, and he goes home to his mother at the break of day. He is the only child-thing among a lot of men who feed on nerves after midnight; and his big, pathetic eyes and cheerful face rebuke all impatience or bad language. He has never known anything but a print shop and his mother, and has had no experiences that were treasurable until the foreman took him fishing and he connected with the eel. After the quick, sharp wrestle on the side of Briar Creek the devil laid down his can of worms and his short pole with the twine string attached and plodded back to the office. 'Rastus was his sub for the night, but for three hours the devil and his eel exercised the prerogatives of the managing editor with right of way over

Associated Press stuff and murder specials. In all his young life this was the first time that the devil had done anything that attracted attention. He was the central figure in the shop, which congratulated him as heartily as if he had sand-bagged a whale, and he was so thoroughly happy that he almost cried. The eel travelled everywhere in the building--was dragged through the coal dust down stairs, came in cold, clammy touch with editorial copy, and at one time was in imminent danger of being devoured by a linotype machine; but the fish and the devil came off triumphant. They finally went out on the streets to be saluted by the hack drivers and the policemen, who know the devil and his people. And everybody was gracious enough to say that of all the eels that were ever caught in the whole world, nobody had ever caught such a grand specimen as that carried by the devil.

It was a big, beautiful night for the devil, and he revelled in his fame. At 4 o'clock in the morning he was curled up in a chair in front of the restaurant with the eel stretched across his knees. His hand clutched the stiffened body, and as he dozed he waked now and then to gaze with rapture into dead fish eyes. At the first streak of day the devil trudged home to his mother, with the calm of a great peace surging through his tired, elated body.

The Reporter's Problem

The city editor of the New York Sun was once asked to define news. After some thought he said:

"If a dog with a tin can tied to his tail runs down Broadway the incident is worth only a few lines, but if a dog with a tin can tied to his tail walks down Broadway the thing is worth a column."

You see the idea. 'Tis the unusual happening that is attractive in the news world; and, certainly, the action of the four young women was unusual enough.

Beg pardon for talking shop; but did you ever think about the disadvantages of trying to write interesting stuff in a place like this? Oh,

Charlotte is a good, big town, and the living here is probably more interesting than in any other place in the South of the same size, but there is very little that transpires here day after day that is important enough to demand scare head lines. For days the bottom drops out of everything. Bill Jones goes to Greensboro on a business trip. Dr. Stagg returns to Birmingham. The recorder catches a crapshooter. The gentleman who had his appendix removed is improving gradually. Crops are worse than ever. Somebody buys a gold mine. Delicious refreshments were served at another party. More about the union depot. You know how it runs, don't you? It's orful. There are no assignments as there are in the big cities. Nobody considerately murders anybody else, and people simply won't embezzle or elope often enough. Yet, in the face of all this, the reporter has got to stump around and rack his brain in kicking up something that will interest somebody.

The test is keener and meaner than in the big cities. Leg work allows a man to exhaust the news field without overmuch difficulty, and then he has to see in happenings things that other people don't see and build stories out of nothing, or with bare ideas as skeletons.

A cub reporter here is far more interesting than a young hyena. He gets a fresh pad, makes spencerian notes, and after carefully sharpening his pencils he extends welcome to every person who comes to town and sheds a tear over all who depart. He spends an hour in relating that somebody who died has passed away with the tide and was a consistent member of the church and the most beloved man that ever was. Then, the cub reporter, conscious of having done his duty, waits for assignments. Assignments! The only regular kind of assignment that can be given a reporter in a place of this size is to say: "There are 30,000 people here. All of them can talk and some of them think. Mix with them, think on your own account, and keep your eyes very, very wide open." That's the feature of the game here. The system is relentlessly simple. The cub reporter can learn to see or he can't learn to see. He is absorptive or unreceptive; he brings every scattered word or idea into account, or he gets no impression from the life about him. He can fasten on the quality of interest and he can put it on paper, or he can't. By an indefinable standard he defines his own worth, and he will rise or drop out of the game altogether.

Take the four women, for instance. They could not fail to be a downright blessing to a newspaper in a town that is so limited in newspaper opportunities as Charlotte. They were respectable women and pretty, and the minute they passed those men in front of the Central Hotel and said "Good evening!" they were worth a column. They could not have done anything that made them worth less than a scare head and a column. They might have been arrested; they might have escaped arrest; they might have gone up in a balloon; or they might have taken the next car for home, but when they electrified a hundred people by speaking to half a dozen they had earned 1,200 words in a newspaper. Two newspaper men saw the women. One reporter was interested personally and waited for some out-and-out notorious sensation. He was disappointed in this, and when asked for his story about the occurrence replied: "It was nothing. Nothing happened. I couldn't get their names, and they got home all right." He is a good enough man, but his eyes failed to see. The other man, who is using the story for illustration and viewed the whole incident merely as one element in the matter of wage-earning, dropped everything when he saw the women, and from that time until he sharpened his pencil at his desk he formed paragraphs in his head. There was nothing else to do. If the dog walks, walks, mind you, he is worth anything.... The unusual thing had occurred. If Col. Willie Phifer would quit going to Stout-on-the-Seaboard, he would be worth half a column a day. If Osmond Barringer would act like other people, he would be a better space-killer than the cotton market. If Col. Walter Henry wore a shirt-waist instead of his long frock coat, which he is supposed to sleep in, he'd be worth a page.

And, it is repeated, the cub reporter will see or he won't see. Happenings--you can't depend upon happenings. In the long, wearisome run everything depends just upon the seeing, the understanding and the telling. Red Buck's brother Bob was up in Huntersville a few years ago and he was moved to emulate Red Buck and write a piece for the paper. He saw two snakes fight, and one of the belligerents, a king snake, throttled the other snake. Quoth Bob in a cramped, boyish hand: "That king snake certainly done his duty." The communication called for an editorial and a statement from the Old Man that Bob could go on the free list for five years if he wanted to. Bob had blundered on something unique, and, no matter if he had blundered, he deserved his reward. Red Buck himself has won success in the reportorial world because his restless eyes are always open to see and he analyzes closely the utterance of every man.

Unprintable Happenings

The impulse to write things that should not be written is one of the most fearsome problems in the newspaper business. Murders, hangings, hotel building, tea parties, fights, industrial deals--these and a lot of other matters that are told in the open are chronicled as a matter of course, but the newspaper man pauses, trembling, before the things that happen and yet are discussed in a whisper.

These are the subjects that you lower your voice to speak of, and you know that if what you were saying were overheard by a certain person you might get your head cracked. Not that you are alone in your knowledge--oh, no. You are quite sure that a lot of men and half the women in town are telling the rest of the population the same sensational story that is related in your undertone.

Talk of this kind might make a lurid, scare-head story, but, usually, it cannot be touched even with a single guarded sentence. Here enters the possible temptation of the newspaper man. The writer has heard in the club or hotels or elsewhere talk on matters that made his hair bristle with excitement, and then he has had to come here and write that the chamber of commerce had postponed its meeting to some other night or that Col. Willie Phifer had spent yesterday at Stout-on-the-Seaboard. He didn't crave to publish scandal or risque gossip, but he knew a thing or two that would interest everybody, and he had to tell a tale that might interest nobody.

The unprintable happenings would be read by the world, no matter if the world's eyes protruded in horror, and nobody knows this any better than a newspaper man. Sometimes the danger line between the questionable and the unquestionable is not clearly defined, and in the hurry of a print shop there must occasionally come an inclination to err in favor of sensation. The writer is positive that he could get out one issue of this paper that would be read and re-read by everybody in the country, but he would never assist in getting out another issue. He'd be killed by a dozen or so different people, though all that he had written would have been true.

Of course this would be going the limit, but this side of that there are all sorts of pitfalls and dangers. The public, you know, thinks that a man on a newspaper is valued because he knows what to write, but the truth is, he holds his job because he ordinarily knows what not to write. A paragraph below this would contain a dozen lines, could relate an occurrence and a living truth that would cause 30,000 people to sit right straight up and jabber all at once, but the writer would demand a clean, fair start for the other side of the world before that paragraph was printed.

Once a paper owned a cub reporter who found nothing in the law building, court house or depots, and then he listened to the uppermost topic of conversation at the square. He came to the shop and wrote what he had heard--a lot of simple facts that would have sold more papers than the burning of the Central Hotel. The story was killed, but the next article by the reporter, which averred that the price of cotton seed in the local market was rapidly rising, was duly published in the paper. The reporter is no longer here. He didn't know the difference between printable and unprintable stuff, and therefore he was more dangerous than a dynamite bomb.

Ideas? Imagination? No use! All gone with the heat. A story that seemed clever a while ago proved as intractable as Mr. D. Allen Tedder's comical tale about a sensation at the Young Peoples' Baptist Union meeting. Another lynching, or an elopement, or a sizable fight at the square--any of these would have been such a boon, but there was an absolute lack of enterprise. . . . Did you ever pick up a pen and write half a sentence, and then rest your face on your hand and dream about nothing in the world--or at least nothing that is writable or printable? Well, it's like that here--now. Speaking confidentially, these words are just space-killers. One of two things is sure to happen inside the next two minutes. The writer will either become reckless and write something that he knows he ought not to write and has been crazy to write for two weeks, or else he will avoid temptation by strolling over and asking the Old Man to walk to the restaurant and have a pie.

"Words, Words, Words"

A poem in yesterday's Observer dealt critically with a certain class of adjectives that are overworked for social purposes, and was in the nature of a plea for new descriptive words to take the place of "function," "dainty," "delicious," "delightful," and other pink-tea terms. As a protest against tiresome iteration the poem took safe ground for criticism, but it did not suggest--for it could not suggest--substitutes for the hackneyed words. The burden of the wearisome repetition falls most heavily upon the reporter, and yet a correct use of his own tools leaves him helpless in the rut. There must be a "function" as a synonym for party, entertainment or reception, and all of these must, in one way or another, be dainty, or delightful, or delicious, or charming. There must be "beauty" in a wedding; grace in every bride; the ceremony must be impressive; and the presents must be numerous and handsome. "Pleasure" and "enjoyment" are as inevitable as smilax and candelabra. In the social department of a paper, the worn words must move in a circle, doing service overtime and wherever men and women gather in dress clothes. The terms are fixed as fate, as inexorable as the laws of nature, and they do duty at the banquet of the princess and at the Sunday dinner party of the milkmaid.

It is not given to the writer of social items to do original or sincere work habitually. Occasionally a spectacular entertainment of the Bradley-Martins in New York or a new-game party in the smaller towns allows latitude and imported platitudes in description, but "en règle" and "fin de siècle" and "recherché" are by-the-way pyrotechnics, and for nearly all time in a big cycle the reporter's pencil is pointed at--just "charming" and "delicious" and "delightful."

A dead line blocks the way out of the thralldom of words. Through long usage the adjectives must continue in use; and it is a daring spirit who is simple and direct in his phrase. When Mrs. B., a prominent society woman, entertains, it may be presupposed that she gave a course dinner, that everybody had enough to eat, and that pleasure was rampant, yet these things must be said, and in saying them it is not easy to bar words like "charming," "delightful," "dainty." The reporter may seek for other verbiage, he may cudgel his poor brain for tricks of inversion and novel, piquant speech, but in the long run his intellect will be socially swamped and "charming" will again rise up and rest before "function."

And why not? Why not welcome the old words--dear, social levellers which bless the hospitality of the rich and the poor alike? "The bride, fair to see, wore a diamond sunburst, the gift of the groom. She looked regal, charming, graceful, winsome. . . ." Let them all stand. The only proper way to tell a thing is the simplest way, and yet the world looks leniently upon a speech that must make every "personality" "delightful" and every "function" a "decided social success." And "charming"? Why, "charming" is the best of the lot; it is so easy, so natural, to say "She looked charming as she recited her marriage vows," or "She gave a charming card party," or "We hope that the charming young lady from Concord will visit the city again ere long." Aren't these averments all right? Mr. Mantalini, the most "delicious" of social frauds, always played a trump card when he called a woman a "demned chawmer."

There comes to memory the pitiable fate of one reporter who sought to be too simple and original. Describing the costumes that were worn at a big party, he said: "Mrs. A. had on nothing that was remarkable." The printer man found a period too many, and the sentence appeared in the paper: "Mrs. A. had on nothing. That was remarkable."

The Comment Man

Certainly hope you won't think anything personal is intended, any way. The writer is tired of being jacked up about abstract pleasantries. Once he ventured to say something in a jesting way about the particular brand of society that likes to nibble oranges on the streets, and the next day he got icy glares from half a dozen people who had really learned to eat ice cream with a fork and olives without a fork several years ago. Words--poor, misused and misunderstood words--are ever falling about and striking in the wrong place, causing hearts to quake or grow hot; and half the universe, thinking on idle speech, curses the other half all the time. Generalities become personalities in a sermon, or on a printed page, or after passing the second mouth on the streets, and you can't be an independent pigmy and slur at mankind without getting the credit of trying to jab the pruning fork into your neighbor around the corner. And, verily, that's what you are trying to do no matter how much you may deny it. No man ever uttered a general criticism without remembering the color of another man's eyes. All Athenians are liars, say you, and you see only Bill Athenian, who said a malicious thing about you. Life is a poor, weary game and people are tiresome, say you, and through the immovable mist you are gazing upon the faint outline of one woman--and only one woman.

"Copy all In"

"No big, pompous tombstones, no high-sounding epitaphs for me," said A. B. Williams, editor of The Richmond News-Leader. "All I want'em to put above my head is:

"'Copy all in.'"

To me that expresses everything--the end of the game. You know what it means, of course. At the end of so many weary, weary nights I have scrawled the words as the finale of toil and as the good-by to my men. 'Copy all in'--and sleep! That is all--the last of life, and then--the rest.

CHAPTER II
CHARLOTTE AND HER NEIGHBORS

A View from the Tower

The thing to do for the stranger within the gates is to betake him to the tower of the D. A. Tompkins Company building. The citizen of Charlotte who thinks he has kept pace with its growth and knows how big the town is ought to go up there and have his eyes opened. The big, square structure, with observatory platform under its very roof, holds its head above all the steeples and domes in the city. It looks high from the street, but a realization of its loftiness is to be gained only by a trip to its top, and really the ascent to the Tompkins tower is one of the treats of Charlotte.

The tower is equal in height to a fourteen-story building and the ascent up to within four floors of the top is made by an electric elevator. All visitors desiring to make the ascent are met by a polite official in the store room on the first floor, where they register their names. There an attendant is assigned them, who accompanies them to the elevator and to the top and designates all the interesting objects in the landscape.

The view from the tower is an extraordinarily fine one. North, south, east and west, it covers every street and house in Charlotte, and the suburban towns are as plain as pictures on canvas. Out over the town on all sides the range of vision extends for distances, varying according to topography, from twelve to thirty miles. One building near Davidson College is clearly indicated, as are also farmhouses about Sharon church. The view of the mountains is surprisingly fine. Not only are a dozen or more individual peaks clearly outlined, but back of them and towering high, but in a paler blue, is seen the Blue Ridge range. The peaks and the range are visible to the naked eye.

The best view of the mountains is to be obtained in the forenoon, when the sun shines upon them, but at any hour of the day the view from the Tompkins tower is an interesting one. At first the visitor is struck with the oddity of the roof effect of Charlotte, and next with the intensified volume of the roar of traffic. The bang and rattle of a loaded truck passing in the street below seems tenfold greater at this height than it does on the street level. The clatter of horses' hoofs and the exhaust of steam engines come up with piercing keenness.

The charm of the view, however, is the picture of moving life, the living current of people and vehicles, the smoke from the factories and the exhaust of the railroad engines on the four sides of the town. The long, curved trestle from Fourth street to Mint street, with the shifting engines going to and fro over it, is strikingly like a section of elevated railroad. In whatever direction one looks, the horizon is blotted with factory smoke. Closer in on the north, south, east and west the black puffs from railroad engines is pierced by the ascending columns of exhaust steam. A beautiful picture of a busy and thrifty city is framed in the white and black of the steam and smoke of industry.

This view of Charlotte and surrounding country is entrancing in itself, but if the visitor happens to be in the tower in the late afternoon, there is injected in the landscape to the south something that is worth looking at. It is the coming of the local train from Atlanta. If the afternoon is still, there will be seen on the western horizon, rounding King's Mountain, a puff of black smoke which slowly rises, spreads and hangs in the air. Then another will rise in front of it, and a short distance nearer still another. That is the trail of the incoming train. The black smoke is emitted as the train is coming up the grades, and when it is first seen the cars are perhaps two miles in front of it. The course of the train can be outlined by the overhanging clouds of smoke until suddenly the engine darts into view through the deep cut on the Dowd farm two miles distant. It is down grade there, and the train comes flying into sight with black smoke and white steam streaming back like ribbons over the roofs of the cars. In a few seconds the whole train comes into view as it crosses the big trestle to the west of the city, then it is alternately hidden as it goes through cuts and under the foliage of trees, until three blocks away it is seen creeping into the train yard. For many minutes after it has reached the depot the route of the train is outlined in the western skies by a lazily rising, sinuous cloud of smoke. The Charlotte citizen who has not been on top of the Tompkins tower does not know Charlotte at all.

The Earmarks of a City

The unconscious action of the inhabitants, and not a flattering census or a few more millions in investments, indicates the transformation of a place from a town into a city. By virtue of certain unmistakable tokens Charlotte has passed through the transition stage and has become a sure-enough city. A strange woman wearing a Parisian gown, her body at a forward incline of forty-five degrees, and a poodle in evening dress, may parade the streets without causing a block in traffic or bringing all the shopkeepers to their windows. Recently a revival and a ball were in progress on the same night; and the city officials do not drop their work and follow a brass band. Residents who travel abroad and return are no longer surrounded at the square and eagerly questioned about the private life of the King or the Pope. Each street offers, without undue vanity, tailor-made and hand-embroidered exhibits; and a whole week, instead of a day, may be required to carry a choice bit of scandal into every part of the town. And the preachers no longer attend courts; plenty of people stay away from funerals; you may dodge a creditor for days without remaining in hiding; the country mules do not shy at automobiles or silk hats walking around on week days; every other woman doesn't speak to every other baby that she meets, and no one thinks about fainting when a Charlotte woman goes off to get a Ph.D. vocal degree and comes home singing in a high Dutch or broken Eye-talian. In fine, Charlotte has all the ear-marks of a city.

Excursionists

The excursionists had possession of the town last week and, apparently, were the happiest people in the place. Most of them came from the thinly settled wayback districts, and when they landed here they found novelty and pleasure in each step of investigation. They fixed a new valuation on the street cars and on the smooth excellence of the macadamized roads; they inspected the old Spanish cannon in front of the post office with greedy curiosity; in pleased way they clustered around the iron slab at Independence Square; they read, with eager interest, the names on the monument in front of the court house; they gazed with awe upon the ponderous proportions of Col. Tom Black, of the police force; they became satiated epicures at the soda fountains; and they returned home tired but filled with content.

One was allowed to see the perfect excursion, which can never leave a city or carry city folks. The ideal excursionist owns no Panama hat or private bath tub, and he is unacquainted with the fascination of a highball. He demands nothing as of right and has no unflattering comparison to make; and he is delighted and satisfied with all he sees and gets. He is youthful, with the chief capacity for tending cows, or he is the toiling head of a household, with scant knowledge of the world outside his own country. The excursion represents a new phase of living or marks an epoch in his life; it stands for a great want that comes but seldom in a lifetime; and the dusty ride and the sights and the strange multitude at the end of the journey appease the want and fill the traveler with new sensations and impressions.

To fully appreciate the joys of an excursion one must have lived in a small town and owned a very particular best Sunday suit of clothes. Then an excursion is glorified like Christmas, and, anticipating it, the blood quickens in the veins and sleep does not come easily. The excursionist goes forth with the pleasure-heart, and no untoward event can debar perfect happiness. He is healthy enough to feel the great Want, and the hurly-burly and unfamiliar excitements gratify the simple bigness of his wish. The denizens of the place that he visits may look upon him in an amused or compassionate way, but he knows, and the gods know, that he is blessed by the gods. If the pleasure that he found right here were infectious the whole town would fall to laughing and shaking hands, and there would be token of the millennium of peace and good-will. An excursion is a twentieth-century trip to Wonderland, which offers weariness and boredom to the inhabitants only.

Cosmopolitanism

You notice that Charlotte people are going to Europe. For a long time they did most of their sightseeing in New York, but ten or fifteen years ago a resident spent three months in Germany and came back speaking broken English, and in recent years another resident returned from England, saying, "I seen the Queen." Since then the exodus to Europe has been steady, and it is singular that as travel increases there is less talk in Mecklenburg of the wonders of the foreign lands. The grand trip has become a matter-of-fact, every-day sort of a proposition, and the village query, "What did you see while you were gone?" seldom has birth here. But the injection of a be-travelled cosmopolitan element into the community is already doing good. It strikes a blow at conceit, narrowness and the provincialism that is satisfied to sit eternally in a small area and judge surely and dogmatically the world and the things of the world. Every man who is not a fool is a better citizen after he goes far enough from his bailiwick to realize his smallness and utter ignorance.

Mr. Roosevelt In Charlotte

The scene at the depot when the President's train pulled in was an animated one. The crowd filled the train yard from end to end, and the number of ladies present was a conspicuous feature. Although ample notice had been given of the coming of the President's train, no arrangement had been made for his reception by the depot people. It was the same old Southern depot, with baggage and express trucks here and there, cars standing on the tracks in the yard, and the same dim, dingy and gloomy lights casting their shadows over it all. When the President's train came to a stop, the rear coach was far below the depot and several detached passenger coaches were on a track alongside of it. The crowd had to squeeze between these cars and the President's coach, and an immovable jam ensued. Only the few who could crowd into the narrow space were fortunate enough to either see or hear the President.

Mr. Roosevelt went to the rear platform as soon as his train came to a stop and seemed to take in the situation at a glance. He leaned out and looked forward over the great mass of people. Holding his silk hat in his right hand and waving command with his left, he said: "Now come along here, quick. You people who are in front move around this way to the rear and right of the car. Move along! Step lively! That's it!" The crowd surged about until the President saw that there was not a foot more of space. "Well," he said, "this seems to be about the best I can do. I am afraid if I keep on I'll spend all my time trying to get the crowd arranged and not get to saying anything, after all."

"What about the Mecklenburg Declaration of Independence?" some one in the crowd shouted.

Quick as a flash, and in tones as clear as a bell, came the response: "The Mecklenburg Declaration of Independence is all right."

"Ladies and gentlemen," continued the President, "I cannot express the pleasure it has given me to meet the people of the South, and I can scarcely find words to express my appreciation of the reception that has been accorded me. Some one has just now asked me what I think of the Mecklenburg Declaration of Independence. Here in Charlotte was made the first Declaration of Independence ever made in the United States." The President then spoke of the spirit that animated the people of this section in the early days of the country and of the part they took in the revolutionary struggles. He praised the patriotic spirit of the South as evidenced in the Spanish-American war, and singled out North Carolina as worthy of particular credit. "In Charleston yesterday," he said, "I reviewed your provisional regiment of troops, and it was as fine a body of soldiers as I ever saw."

Just at this point the President's train began moving out. Abruptly breaking off his speech, he shouted so that almost everybody in the train yard could hear: "I want to say this: During the Cuban campaign I once had occasion to select twenty sharpshooters. Two of the twenty were North Carolinians!"

These were the President's final words. As the train pulled out, Mr. Roosevelt leaned over the railing of the platform, waving his hat and bowing. Mrs. Roosevelt stood by his side, smiling in thorough delight at the cordiality of her husband's reception in Charlotte.

In Sunday Clothes

Standing at the square yesterday in the forenoon, one saw nearly all Charlotte going to church. 'Twas a grand sight--a well-dressed multitude. The place is still small enough for every one to know the Sunday clothes of every one else; and yesterday there was a pleasant rustle of new silks and the creak of new shoes. Sunday clothes! They're martyrdom up to fifteen years of age; an embarrassment until 20; a joy until 30; and after that just a necessity and a disillusionment. Sunday clothes mean the big, hallowed moments of youth and the philosophy of the after years. The light-gray suit is as the vital presence of the fresh glories of springtime, the quick-pulsed blood and the faint perfume of a slender girl's hair; but the light-gray suit blushes under the cool glare of the long, dark, dignified coat, which has ceased to garb pleasure and vanity and looks scornfully on the pampering of frail tabernacles. Sunday clothes pick up the happiness that is lost when one ceases to go barefooted; they contain or reflect the rarest happiness until eyes lose lustre, and then Sunday clothes go to funerals--all sorts of funerals.

But--

"Manhood has no joys so lustrous;

Nothing that so gladsome seems--"
As the first pair of trousers.

Music at the Club

The Southern Manufacturers' Club in this city is making some odd experiments in music. It has a piano and a Cecilian, and gets pretty much all the latest music by a system of swapping old tunes for new tunes. About fifty members of the club keep the Cecilian working from 8 o'clock in the morning until 11:30 at night. It has been discovered that everybody gets tired of even the best pieces of modern music in about ten days. The members have run the gamut of all the light operas, ragtime music, and the most celebrated output of modern composers, and always retire each of these inside a fortnight. Isadore Rush sang "Egypt," and the club sent a special delivery for that song. It was played 704 times the first day it arrived, a fortnight ago, but was played only once yesterday. This week "Egypt" will die. In a word, the Southern Manufacturers' Club, a representative organization of this cultured section, has decided that no piece of music that has been written in the last four or five years is worth living. The Cecilian has tried almost everything, and it has made that piano do more hard work than any other piano ever did in a quarter of a century. Up there where a man betrays a soulful expression by the movement of the muscles in the calves of his legs, only three pieces of music have been selected to live, the "Intermezzo," "La Paloma," and "The Last Rose of Summer."

Beds of Violets

In front of the residences on the principal streets--or all the streets--in this city there are living violet beds; and it is to be hoped that the town will never grow so large or so citified as to prevent the growing of these tender, country violets right in its very heart. They are, in some way, a symbol of daintiness, freshness, purity. They best become a maiden or a womanly woman, and they are a silent rebuke to a woman who is bad. And one knows, somehow, that a woman who goes out and fusses over violet beds and really loves the little human things has the right kind of a soul. There is no reason for saying this; it is another one of the just-so things. All other flowers are-- flowers, but violets grow and whisper in the innocent realm that can only be seen by a baby's eyes and are the first offering in the kingdom where love must give the right gift to love.

Small Towns

The small towns in this State are interesting affairs. People living in them have such an unlimited amount of things to talk about. In the bigger places folk sometimes get tired of conveying intelligence to other folks, but in little towns people cease conversation only when they go to bed. It is a very happy existence. One may be tired for a while, but after the first few months he whittles sticks with the rest of the population and becomes a fixture. Wentworth, down in Rockingham county, is an ideal hamlet for that sort of thing. Wentworth surrendered to Cornwallis and fought Cotton Mather's doctrines, but since then other men have surrendered to Wentworth and have garnered cobwebs and lived in peace. Right now in Wentworth there are men who sit around open fires with their coats off who might be running the Government or assisting Panama. In Wentworth and larger North Carolina towns there is such an incessant amount of matters to get excited about, apart from the growth of weeds in court-house yards or an unfortunate remark that was dropped at a Sunday-school social. This is no criticism of small towns. Bless them all! They breed the biggest men, the rarest news, and the biggest liars. And such love is awakened in small-town citizenship! What is Boston to Hillsboro, Paris to Morganton, or St. Petersburg to Lincolnton? What is a metropolis compared to a town where one has speaking acquaintance with every dog that he meets, knows every face in a congregation, and is permitted to add his hush-note to the last dear song of gossip. The privileges of a small town are many and each one has an interrogation point after it. But when you're sick, they all send you things to eat, and when you die the heartfelt sob is heard above the wail of the little organ. One would go back to the small town just as the stag goes back to die at the place he was 'roused.

Lincolnton

Lincolnton need not get worried over being called sleepified. A compliment was intended. The Lincolnton people have plenty of money and cotton mills and enterprise, and they can lead the universe in cooking beaten biscuits; but the town is sleepified just the same. Nice sleepified! There are no end of moss-covered wells there, and shade trees and vine-covered porches; there is an insectish drone in the atmosphere; a mule standing in front of the post-office drops into slumber; the voice of a woman calling a child arouses one like a challenge and can be heard a mile; a gentleman from the country tilts his chair against the side of a store and snores. That's Lincolnton--bless it! Stay there a month and time may hang heavily on your hands; stay there two months and you never want to live anywhere else. When you're well, everybody knows what you have to eat; when you're sick, everybody sends you things to eat. That's Lincolnton--dear, old sleepified Lincolnton.

Taylorsville

The new court-house at Taylorsville, Alexander county, will have no bell. The old court-house has a bell, which the writer has previously emphasized as the most interesting bell in North Carolina. Formerly that bell rang whenever a beef was killed--rang out the tidings of salutations and felicitations. The residents of the community might be drowsing of a peaceful summer day, but when the bell pealed forth there was a sudden and remarkable activity as all hands sprinted to view the cow that had died; and, as the residents ran, many were the joyous bets as to whether the late deceased was a heifer or a plain, unvarnished bull yearlin'. With the next court-house that dear old bell will go forever--alas! An Alexander cow must die silently, with a bitter tear in her eye.

Circus Day

All of the circus was not under canvas.

The day was unusual. It was, as Col. Tom Black predicted, a record-breaking circus day. Fourteen thousand people saw the afternoon performance, and such attendance was considered marvellous, even in a city where the circus numbers its devotees from the oldest to the youngest member of every household.

And certainly 10,000 people--and may be 20,000 people--got drenched--not wet after the usual fashion, but wet in a cosy, complete way that caused the proud crests of women's hats to droop soggily, sent their bedraggled skirts under their heels as they walked, and caused the color of a man's hat to show in the hurrying raindrops as they fell from the tip of his nose.

Bunched in front of the circus tent were the besoaked; bunched they were in town; and betwixt and between they scurried like so many dismal, rain-reeking sheep, or like a multitude of principals who were returning from a colossal baptizing.

Such is a cursory view of the main features of yesterday in Charlotte.

In gala day attire and mood Charlotte turned out en masse, but Charlotteans were hardly to be recognized in the scurrying throng. In a night and a day a new population had sprung up; had come here on trains, in carriages, wagons, and in all manner of vehicles; had walked here. Strangers strolled familiarly on the streets, and took major part in the festivities. They came from all near-by towns and from distant places; and they appeared in silk hats, in celluloid collars, and in the homespun clothes that mark the mountaineers from Yancey, Mitchell, Wilkes, and other mountain counties. The city had lost its complexion. It was a mere bump on the earth where humanity disported itself like a seething mass of ants, and forgot dull care in a thirst for a sight of the elephant and Pierrot gambolling in the aroma of clean, sweet sawdust.

By daylight the visiting gentlemen from Bakersville, Burnsville, and North Wilkesboro had fed their horses and had taken positions where they might get an undisturbed view of the grand parade. The great majority of these came here just to see the parade; rode the best part of two days and suffered the inconvenience of camping out to enjoy the pleasure of seeing their lordships the lion and the kangaroo ride past in stately splendor and to sit in critical judgment upon the new melodies that were to be wafted from the steam piano. To them the parade was the beginning and end of all things wonderful. Fifty cents meant admission into the Place Beautiful, where the monkey claims a lawful and honorable place in man's estate, and where a woman, who stands on one foot on a flying horse and kisses the tips of her fingers, may become a more enduring vision than the most fantastic conception of beauty that might come to one who stood on Pisgah's top and saw heaven in the majesty of the rolling clouds.

So visitors from the backwoods districts and thousands of others waited only on the feast that came with the parade and found therein satisfaction to the utmost.

By nine o'clock dense crowds of people lined the thoroughfares along the length of South Tryon street and down North Tryon street as far as Ninth street. The crowd thickened, and yet more people came out to wait and see. At eleven o'clock traffic along the line of march was almost completely blocked. At the square men touched elbows on every foot of space. Sidewalks, bulging with humanity, thrust loads into the streets, and every porch, every window, every veranda was packed.

Good nature was everywhere manifested. The day was unseasonably warm, and men jostled one another at every step, and yet the spirit of jollity was writ large on every face, and laughter rang out above the hum of conversation.

The parade, coming shortly after noon, brought the noiseless appreciation that betokens success. There was no applause. "Going to see a circus," remarked the Old Man, "is like periodical drinking. No man would care to see a circus two days running, but once a year the world gets hungry for the sight of a clown."

And so, along the long line, there was the quick gasp of delight that surcharged the atmosphere. The eyes of the aged citizen glistened; the face of the little boy radiated silent joy. The clown was as glorious as the bearded king who rode on his chariot, and who, indeed, would have been bold enough to choose between a bear and a red brass band?

The show did not begin until two o'clock, but an hour and a half before that time an army of people began entrance into the portals of the big canvas. The crowd adjusted itself perfectly and never seemed to get in its own way; and which the large first tent containing the animals and the free attractions was full at all times before the performance began, yet the congestion was constantly being relieved by the tide that swept on and deposited its human freight in the spacious ampitheatre.

But the reporter paused and communed with the animals and lingered to hear the words that fell from the lips of the bearded lady.

The parade indicated what the menagerie of Barnum & Bailey's would be. It is solid--as solid as wealth and wide experience can devise--as solid, in point of instruction, as a book on natural philosophy. There were no frills. There were monkeys, but not enough monkeys to raise unseemly chatter, while there were not too many remnants of extinct species to arouse suspicion. The six and twenty elephants fixed the standard for the menagerie. Everything was elephant-strong and elephant-good--good as twenty-carat gold--good enough to check levity and bring sober, respectable interest to a sea of faces.

The reporter drifted with the crowd and cursed bitterly because he was denied the gift to paint the fresh, human pictures that faced him wherever he looked.

The animals inside the cages deserved the attention given by those outside. After satisfying his curiosity, one passed by the Red River hog of West Africa and the Collar bear from Thibet, and paused in front of the cages that held the trained lions from Nubia and the tigers from India. The sight of these lions alone was worth the price of admission. They were grave, stately beasts, not fussy, but dignified, gazing into nothingness with a far-away expression in their eyes. Their severe demeanor seemed to rebuke the fretfulness of the puma and others of the lesser cat tribe who roamed up and down in near-by cages. The lion--one of nature's few perfect-looking creatures--made all things human under the canvas look feeble, ineffectual. Such majesty towered there, finding strange harmony in the tiger's sinuous grace--in that incarnation of suggestive and actual beauty.

The crowd wavered, and broke, and went on, but one figure stood silently in front of the cage of the hippopotamus. This was Col. Henry C. Cowles, of Statesville, whose love for the hippopotamus has been previously adverted to in this paper. Living nearly always in Iredell county, Colonel Cowles has a natural liking for a mule; he fancies a good horse; he is fond of a dog; and has affection for a good cow; but since he was a boy he has selected the hippopotamus as an animal upon which he lavishes a wealth of interest and affection. "Samantha," said a countryman on one occasion to his wife, "this is the hippopotamus cow, and my! ain't she plain?" But Colonel Cowles finds only beauty lines in the broad, wet back and sees tenderness and domestic traits in the expansive countenance of the large animal. If he had gone no farther than the one big cage, he would have been repaid for his visit to Charlotte yesterday. With enraptured face he watched the keeper feed the hippopotamus on wet bran, and his hand went out involuntarily as if he would wish to stroke the dripping nozzle. "Above all the animals that are," said Colonel Cowles, "give me the hippopotamus cow--the noblest of all the wild beasts in the world."

Every man to his own choice; and Rob Reinhardt, of Lincolnton, and several little Reinhardts who tugged at his hand, foregathered with the camels--just stood and gazed into the eyes of the herd of camels and seriously nodded their approval. A man across the way yelled that the albino gentleman would now proceed to throw his backbone out of joint, and even as he spoke the gentleman who has no hands at all began to write a spencerian hand with his two large toes; but Bob Reinhardt only leaned down on the ropes and scrutinized more closely the camels. There was more or less pathos in his expression, and a great deal of dejection in his bearing, as he turned away after a few minutes' conversation with the keeper of the animals. Mr. Reinhardt and the little Reinhardts had failed in their purpose to purchase a camel that they could take back to Lincolnton and drive in a buggy, and hitch to the stake in front of the post-office and thus breed envy into a peaceful hamlet.

There were lots and lots of other animals. Zebras, emus, trained sheep, gnus, kangaroos, antelopes, buffaloes, bears, monkeys--these and others were present. And one giraffe! Tall, slender, graceful he stood--one of the rarest of the wild creatures. "You see, sir," said his keeper, "they don't live long. They get pneumonia, or some other ailment, on the slightest provocation, and they don't stand captivity well. Excepting a female that is in the North and is about to give birth to a little one, this is the only giraffe owned by Barnum & Bailey. Mr. Bailey has a standing offer of $10,000 for a giraffe, and it doesn't seem that the order is to be filled."

Two dozen elephants stood in a semicircle, and across the path stood a mother elephant who munched hay and gazed reflectively upon a baby that had recently become her very own. The elephants are well mannered, and they neither receive nor ask for the edibles that are popularly supposed to be handed out by the small boys and the intoxicated patrons. "There is something pathetic to me about an elephant," said Mr. W. D. Coxey, the genial press representative of the show. "He is a wise fellow and he bears captivity stolidly and sensibly. He is like the Hindoo; he does the best he kin do; and yet I want to cry when I see him, the big, sturdy thing, doing infantile stunts and then walking out of the arena with a subdued expression in his eyes and his trunk fastened around the tail of the elephant in front of him. Yet they get ugly sometimes, and when an elephant does get mean there is but one thing to do with him--kill him. Yes, we have had to kill four in recent years. How? Well, the method is rather unique and almost invariable. We stake the elephant firmly to the ground, pass a long chain around his neck, fasten two stout elephants to each end of the chain, and they become the executioners by a choking process."

The free list attractions in the centre of the tent were attractive up to the point where unsightliness caused something akin to nausea. The programme states that Grace Gilbert, the bearded lady, is gentle, delicate, and intensely feminine in all her characteristics, and yet at the age of twenty-six years she has a beard "of an average of about ten inches." It is also averred that she has refused many proposals of marriage. Poor bearded lady! One saw the well-rounded figure, saw the slender woman's hands, glanced up and imagined the transports of embracing Esau, and turned with relief to the four-hundred-pound fat lady who is the breathing, peaceful image of Charlie McCord.

There was the dear old dog-faced boy. Only they dignify him by calling him the lion-faced boy now. Dear old reminder of childhood's days; furnishing the best term to sneer at ill-favored, unlikable folk. The man with the hard head, the human telescope, Miss Leah May, the American giantess, the living skeleton, the whirling Dervish, the needle-eater and the fire-eater, the albino dislocationist, the human pincushion, Eli Bowen, the legless acrobat, Charles Tripp, the armless wonder--aye, these and more were all there. A rare collection of freaks. A little bit of a boy threw his arm around his father's neck and wept as if his heart would break. "Oh, sonny," said the father, "don't cry. That's only poor old Krao, the missing link." But sonny couldn't reason very clearly about evolution, and every time he and Krao exchanged glances he bawled the louder. One is enlightened to note in the programme that Krao is a she. Most anywhere she would be taken for a he, or a plain, every-day him.

"Just look at the midgets," said Mr. Coxey. "To me they are the most interesting people in the show."

The biggest midget is a woman, shapely, rather pretty. "And quite refined," said Mr. Coxey. "Different? No, she is for all the world just like other women--has the same ideas, the same desires." There were four other midgets; two comparatively tallish little fellows, and two tiny little chaps and the tiniest sort of a little woman. She was dressed in evening costume and had lots of pretty hair that was gracefully arranged. She strolled up and down the platform with her hand on the arm of the smaller of the two littlest midgets, but her eyes kept turning to the larger of the two. "That's a sad case," said Mr. Coxey. "She is crazy about that little fellow. To her he is the biggest, boldest, bravest man in the world. She has been in love with him for a long time. When we were in Budapest last year, they announced their engagement, and a number of us, including some German newspaper men, gave them a pre-nuptial banquet. After the toast of the evening had been made the bridegroom-to-be rose to his feet, and, in responding, said that he was not so sure about being married after all. He said he would have to think it over for a while. What a bombshell his announcement caused, and how that little woman did suffer! But since then they've been getting friendlier, and I fancy the thing will end in marriage. She's quite daffy about him, and to her he is tall and stately and more beautiful and heroic than all the princes of the fairy tales."

The circus itself! What is there to say about a circus? As the years pass they change a bit and grow larger, and yet the essentials must remain the same. Pleasure builded above the sawdust that contains the clown, the elephant, the acrobats, the bareback riders, the long whirl of a body from one trapeze to another, the chariot races--such things are to be the eternal fabric of a circus. Sometimes there is more; sometimes less; always a circus gives better return for money than any other form of amusement. And yesterday it was more. Three pulsing rings made the eyes swim and tired one's brain. The only risk, in pleasure's name, was in surfeit. Four hundred women came out and gave the spectacular "tribute to Balkis," a rhythmic, harmonious spectacle that delighted the eye and pleased the senses. After that--after the end of a gorgeous prelude--event followed event in mad succession, and the spectator was entertained in half a dozen different ways at once. There was an inner cry to stop the thing so that each act could be examined in detail. The elephants were wonderfully clever; the horse-back riding was attractive, if not particularly thrilling; the acrobatic work and the other athletic features, including the exhibition of Japanese jugglers; the tight-rope walking; the beautiful trained horses and dogs, the horse racing and then the chariot racing--all these and the dozens of other features were very good indeed. If one were called upon to select the cleverest part of the show he would at once point to the work of the two aerialists, the Clarkonions, one of whom turns a double sommersault and then turns his body completely round, in mid-air, before catching the arms of the other performer, which hang down from a high trapeze. In a word, the big show had everything that a show ought to have, and it is the most complete circus that has ever visited the South.

"Where do our performers come from?" said Mr. Coxey. "Why, most of them are from England, a good many from Germany, and others from France and Bavaria. The Americans are not as good circus performers, not as good riders or acrobats, as the Europeans. The American temperament is impatient, and the ordinary American hasn't the patience to spend a lifetime trying to learn to do a certain kind of work. And so much as that is required of a circus performer. It is strange enough that most of the midgets and the other freak people come from Bulgaria or Bavaria. Most of our performers are grouped in families. Those seven women who are doing turns in the far ring are French Jewesses--the mother and daughters and cousins. Those in the next ring are a German and his wife and his daughter and her husband. Certain families seem to be producing circus performers. This promotes morality; and a circus is not half so immoral as it is popularly supposed to be. The family idea is strongly opposed to anything wrong, and I'll tell you another thing: It is the lazy life which contains no exercise that leads oftenest to physical wrong-doing. Where you find a lot of people who must keep sober and are continually taking a lot of the right sort of exercise you are not apt to find vice or viciousness."

There was a start of surprise, and the show was over. The concert was a whit better than the usual catchpenny aftermath; and the side show owns one exhibit alone that is worth going many miles to see. This is the giant--the best looking and the biggest giant that any one ever saw. He is 7 feet 9 inches high, wears a No. 36 shoe, weighs 400 and some odd pounds, and is well proportioned. But he seems to be a most unhappy giant. He creates the impression that he is lonesome, and a man who makes the sad error of growing to be that big is apt to be more or less lonesome all his days. He conversed with the fat lady and the lady who toys with the reptiles, but he always kept that weary look in his sensible and sensitive kind of eyes. One has an idea that the giant is apt to die an old bachelor, and probably he broods about the matter. The other things and people in the side show were scarcely worth while, though it is observed that humanity at large does take a morbid sort of pleasure in looking upon ungainly or ghastly sights and malformations that go to make up the exhibits in the conventional side show.

But there is another brief chapter to add to the events of yesterday. This embodied the rain. And such rain! The storm came in a heavy, noiseless down-pour shortly after the show began and held up at intervals during the performance. After the show was over, the people who caught the first cars to town escaped a wetting, but those who were forced to linger almost swam to town. Thousands of people, seeing the congested condition of the street cars, set out to walk to town. Not one man in twenty had an umbrella. The rain fell insidiously, just as if to tempt pedestrians to brave it for a while, and then suddenly it was coming down in torrents. In a few minutes, a thick, straggling line from Latta Park to town was wet to the skin, and then the march to the city was made recklessly. In the space of a mile and a half, probably four thousand women strode in the blinding rain and more than that many men were so badly caught that they could afford to disregard further hurt from the elements. No civilized land ever before presented such an untidy picture.

With outer skirts tucked around their waists, and with white skirts muddied their entire length women splashed through deep puddles, buried their feet in red clay, pushed wet, dishevelled hair back from the eyes, and finally began to laugh and enjoy the adventure. The entire town seemed to be caught unawares. The wave of recklessness seemed everywhere; a sympathetic something that made all men and women dare to walk out and get thoroughly soaked. The stragglers, coming to town, found a bedraggled population wandering hither and thither, taking no thought to protection.

Then all Charlotte--and may be the strangers--undressed and toasted its feet, and put on clean clothes, and declared that the day had been entirely good and that the joyous crowd that was scattered abroad in the local land was even larger than the audience that faced Mr. William Jennings Bryan when he first visited this city. And no one seemed to care because the presence of the Nebraskan had ceased to mark the high ebb of population in the Queen City of the South.

CHAPTER III
CHARACTER SKETCHES

"The Bull of the Brushies"

Ex-Congressman Romulus Z. Linney, of Taylorsville, better known as the Bull of the Brushies, arrived in town yesterday, and will be here for several days. From the time he entered the lobby of the Buford Hotel until he retired last night, he was always surrounded by a crowd; and generally he was the spokesman, though the attentive pricking-up of his ears and the narrow closing of his eyelids indicate that as a listener he is a genius--a man that the world likes to whisper to.

Among all the odd men who are grown on the highland health in western North Carolina, Mr. Linney is the strangest, the most distinctive. Even Dickens never knew his kind, or fashioned a type that is near akin to the Bull of the Brushies. He is older now than he used to be, but his rotund figure is as active as of yore; the eyes just as emotional; the voice as quick and strong, and ready as ever to speak language like that of no other man in the universe.

Most men who read literature hold it in reserve as mere ornate punctuation or emphasis for every-day speech, but Mr. Linney breathes composite rhetoric at breakfast. The cadence of "Locksley Hall," the quaintness and subtle charm of Coke, the common-sense phraseology of John Stuart Mill, the rareness of Shakespeare--all these blend in single sentences when words fall from the lips of this strange man of genius. In congressional halls he has caused laughter by the use of colloquialisms that are his birthright; while in the far-back rural districts he has combined, in furious speech, Spencer, the Old Testament, Bill Nye, Blackstone and the Constitution, and aimed them with telling force at an audience that was moved to weep blind tears.

And he is notable everywhere he goes. You will mark him on the streets if you see him. People in Washington and New York used to turn and gaze upon him; they knew not why. A costly frock coat, the product of an expensive tailor, is on his back, and does not conceal fancy corduroy trousers that are both serviceable and splotched.

Ever since he ceased to be a Democrat, Mr. Linney has been a Republican. That's a way he has of doing things. He is a positive character, and is pretty apt to be one thing or another. Just now he is preparing to obtain the Republican congressional nomination in the eighth district, and he is quietly trying to further his chances by foregathering with the hordes of Republicans who are here in attendance upon the District Court. Mr. Linney explained the matter in another way in answer to a question of the reporter.

"Why do I come here, sir?" he replied. "I come here, sir, to attend a meeting of the patriots; and only Republicans are patriots. I come here, sir, to be present at a love feast; to be an humble factor in a reunion that stirs the soul and warms the heart." He waved his hand benignly over a circle that included Judge Boyd, Gus Price, Mr. S. Wittkowsky, Col. H. C. Eccles and a few others.

"Do I expect to get the nomination in the eighth district? I do. I expect to thunder out the truth to the good people of that district; and I shall expect to defeat for the nomination my friend, Spencer Blackburn.

"Yes, if I am nominated I shall hope to run against Mr. Theo. F. Kluttz. Will that give me pleasure, sir? Pleasure? Why, I will be honored in meeting such an eloquent, courteous gentleman.

"But disturb me not with these minor matters and let me reflect in peace upon the beneficence of that God-fearing citizen, Marcus Hanna. Sir, I look upon him not so much as an ordinary man, but I love to think on the qualities of his great soul. Here hero-worship has no taint of sacrilege. And I may add that my tribute is incomplete without grouping alongside Mr. Hanna two other Christian gentlemen, Grosvenor, of Ohio, and President Theodore Roosevelt. Each challenges hero-worship--receives it. Yes, I think Roosevelt will be the next President."

"What do you think about Judge Boyd's ticket: Roosevelt for President and Judge W. S. O'B. Robinson for Vice-President?"

"Judge Robinson is a brilliant man and is determined to make a reputation for himself," said Mr. Linney, who is a diplomat.

The sublime mood flickered for a moment on the mobile face, and comical curves worked at the corners of his mouth. "Happy?" he said. "Yes, I am happy. You should have been with me, sir, recently. I have been in the Second Paradise, out yonder in Watauga county, on the top of Ritch Mountain, six thousand feet above the level of the sea." Eloquence flashed once again in the merry, passionate eyes, and then died, and the Bull of the Brushies was trailing on the level.

"I have come down here to meet with the clansmen," he said with a grin, "and it reminds me of the rubbing of dead shad together."

The Original Dugger

Prof. Shepherd Monroe Dugger came to the city not with the loud heralding that should have announced his approach, and when he would have lectured in the court-house last evening he found himself facing only a few persons, and therefore he determined to postpone his discourse until Thursday night, when he will speak in the Y. M. C. A.

Professor Dugger is very anxious to speak before a representative Charlotte audience, and it is to be hoped that he will be greeted with a large audience when he rises up to speak on "How to Make Sober Men and Happy Women." The nominal charge of fifteen and twenty-five cents should not be a strong enough barrier to keep any one from tasting the eloquence of the famous author of "The Balsam Groves of the Grandfather."

Professor Dugger is modestly proud of his lecture and the effect that it has had upon residents of Gastonia and upon people in other places where he has been recently. He was permitted to speak in churches, and he said he gave offense to no one, and that people invited him around to dinner and expressed their appreciation of his efforts. "I am not so green at the business as I once was," he said. "I have learned many things since the time I used to lecture up there in the mountains. I can feel how my audience is feeling, and if I am about to go too far I can see the danger in the eyes of the first young woman whose eyes I happen to see."

Prof. Dugger explained that the theme of his lecture was so narrowed that it did not deal with a great variety of subjects. Intemperance in all its branches, the usefulness of honest work, the right sort of domestic life, love, courtship, marriage, and the humor that is injected into side-line jokes--these and just a few other topics are reckoned with in his lecture. "And I am not so crude a stick of material as formerly," asseverates Professor Dugger. Which means that his lecture is a refined thing that will tickle a sensitive palate without causing the least bit of nausea.

His friends here who have seen Shepherd Monroe Dugger on his native heath, standing hard by his beloved Grandfather Mountain and emitting bold, wonderful, weird and volcanic words, entertain the fear that, may be, the fierce, primitive genius has become too softened by the search for refining influence. Has Dugger become tame? That is the question. Is this the same Dugger who said roughly, "I don't want to talk to any audience whose faces look like a carload of bruised watermelons"? That's the Dugger that the people wish to hear; that's the Dugger who won fame that spread to the furthermost confines of the nation. Let him speak further, if he pleases, of the boil on the old lady's back; let him find and hurl to the startled winds more and yet more of his perorations which overwhelm one with terrific unfathomableness. His friends here venture to express the hope that the original and only Duggerism will manifest itself here Thursday night.

Let the professor spout the great clarion lingo that came to him and possessed his soul as he and the Grandfather Mountain slept side by side. Let him do this, and the Charlotte audience, which is ever heroic in patience and courage despite unfair handling, will endeavor to rise to the point of understanding and, even if appalled, will yet be grateful for having heard unadulterated, unlassoed and untamable Duggerism.

There must be no restraint for Prof. Shepherd Monroe Dugger, and this counsel comes at the behest of his friends who have seen him moving and speaking as an untrammelled scion of the Blue Ridge. He now wears a long frock coat and shakes hands rather too high in the air. He refused yesterday to say "ain't," and picks his words with a preciseness that caused nervousness. He claims to be an apostle to intellectual reformation, and the claim causes regret. The great Dugger must not learn away from his early creed and language. Let him say, "My darlin' Mihilda, Mahulday, Mahishla Jane, if you'll allow me to implant upon your cavernous mouth some faint evidence of my inconsiderable ability as an osculatory artist, I'll cure your toothache." Let him say that if he wants to. Let him gurgle as wildly as the raciest mountain stream; let him roar with the untutored majesty of Linville Falls. Break forth, Dugger--be the old Dugger! Howl, sing, lash yourself in the dear old way and make everybody sit up. Fifteen cents "per" entitles the local world to no big demand; but, in the name of Bullscrape and by the sacred beard of the Grandfather, it is your duty to bust loose and warble the same song that used to shake and overturn intellects in the high hills.

With his hair disordered, his cravat askew, and his eye--both eyes--in fine frenzy rolling, Prof. Shepherd Monroe Dugger, lecturer, and author of "The Balsam Groves of the Grandfather Mountain," strolled into The Observer office yesterday and, striking himself on the chest, said loudly:

"The only and original Dugger, the bard of Banner Elk, still lives!

"Read this," said the only authorized spokesman for the Grandfather Mountain--"read this and know that Duggerism still survives." Here was the offering:

"Yesterday's Observer says: 'In the name of Bullscrape and by the sacred beard of the Grandfather it is your duty to bust loose and warble the same song that used to shake and overturn intellects in the high hills.'

"Let me answer my friends in Charlotte that I still possess the lingo that sighs in the balsams of the Grandfather. The Linville Falls are pouring as vividly in my cranium as when I lifted the speckled beauties flaunting in their white spray. The rhododendrons continue to bloom in the horizon of the forests as the borealis of the floral kingdom. Every crystal fountain is a silvery tongue of the mountain bubbling poems from its orifice; pouring torrents, dallying through twisted gyves, steal the hues of the rainbow and paint them on the sides of their fishes, and the blood from angels' wounds, still falling from the battle in heaven, leaves its formula and sad muse upon the autumnal leaves."

As these words were read the fine raiment of the poet of Banner Elk seemed no longer to conceal the strange personality of that Dugger who, as foreman for all the road-working forces in Watauga county, had once proudly termed himself "The Colossus of Roads." With the murmur of such eloquence there was wafted to aroused senses a long, sweet breath from the high hills, the cry of the owl under the moon, the far whisper of gurgling streams, the scent of wet green things.

The old Dugger, the real Dugger, is alive and not dead.

Nat Gray

Once more the theatrical season opens in this city, and the voice of Col. Nathaniel Gray is silent. For many years he was the engineer of the gilded, tinselled art--the manager of the opera house that saw the great Booth and mocked cobwebs and discomfort by the parade of lesser lights. All of talent that came he brought and revelled in. As the proud patron of it all, he laughed for years with Pierrot, sighed with Cinderella, languished with Romeo, and wept with Brutus. So much did his office enter into his daily life that he said "Gadzooks" in the little barber shop that he owns on West Trade street, and he tried to teach his little dog to emulate the proud manner of the distinguished lion that brought fame to the opera house season before last. But the place beautiful is even now almost forgotten. That brilliant curtain with the sixteenth-century figures, the Arabian horses, and the nineteenth-century hotel in the left-hand corner--where is that curtain? Where the spluttering purple lights and pink lights--where the green garden scene that has contained King John, Rupert of Hentzau, Petronius, Hamlet, Richelieu and Wild Bill? Where the sacred seats that witnessed so long the tales of greatness and heroism? Gone! "The wind has blown them away." Swept is the histrionic dust. An eerie sound is there. Ghosts may rehearse by ghostly limelight, and the shade of the princess who wore the imitation silk may curtsey to the king who wore gaiter shoes, that were marked down to $1.98; a Roman legion can appear in misty array, but the spirit of the old house, that so gloated over its changing throng, is dead in silence. The manager is out of business. Retired! He raises chickens in Utopia--which is Dilworth. Raises chickens and beets--and things. And so finds happiness for a later life. Out into the darkness he looks peacefully, hopefully. Close to nature he is; the keen, sweet breath of the forest is wafted to him; he hears the last tuneful carol of the lark at eventide; he looks deep into the eyes of the youthful chickens, and finds rest, surcease of sorrow. It is given to him, even as it is given to Col. Jeems Howie, to know the blessings of the quieter living; to know that in ruraldom poverty is as precious as affluence. Here, he knows, all men must live alike. And he has found, as Colonel Howie found, that--

"Them that has no hired hands blows the dinner horn just the same as them that has."

Kid Sloan

Kid Sloan died yesterday afternoon at 4:30 o'clock at St. Peter's Hospital. The cause of his death was alcoholism. It would be no kindness to Kid to try to let him down light by saying that he died from some other sickness. As he had anticipated, he passed out the liquor way, and if he had any voice in the matter now he would sneer at an effort to disguise the truth.

This history of Kid Sloan--or David Wilson Sloan--was published in The Observer a few days ago. He was a waif who was hurled around the world laughingly but violently. He knew nothing but a print shop and humanity, and he knew both well. He was thirty-eight years of age--old in experience, young at heart, and one of the swiftest compositors in the United States.

Kid was born in Stanly county, but he had lived in almost every part of America, and he knew the manners and sayings of many peoples. In a Bohemian sense he was a thorough man of the world and his fund of anecdote was enormous. He absorbed color at every point he touched and put it to no use except to amuse his friends. He had lost the faculty of being surprised at anything in the world, but his sense of humor kept him blithe and fresh until his being was finally engulfed in rum. After his death it is remembered that he was the quaintest and the most interesting personage in the town. He accomplished nothing that was worth while, but he was utterly fascinating.

Kid was a morphine fiend, an opium fiend, and a drunkard, but he never did a mean or a malicious thing in his life. He was the sort of a man who would pick up a strange, friendless dog and carry it home and give it half of his last crust. He never had much to give, but he was always perfectly willing to give all that he had. When his body writhed bitterly with the torture of self-punishment, he yet radiated laughter. He was ever the chiefest figure in every group that opened to receive him, and, no matter what hell he placed upon his own soul, he spent the best part of his thirty-eight years in giving mirth that was sweet and wholesome by essence and strength. No man who ever met Kid Sloan can forget him--can forget that tiny, warped form or the droll, incisive speech that fell from the thin, seamed lips. Kid might have been an eastern philosopher transplanted. He was out of place here--a weird little personality that understood everything about and was never understood; a pitiful little chap who laughed and made others laugh, harmed no one but himself, and died without ever having grieved or lost a friend.

Kid would have understood this obituary, for he liked plain speech and hated "slopping over." He never lied about anything and he shall not be lied about.

The immediate particulars relating to his death are briefly told. He used morphine and cocaine for many years, and there was hardly a part of his body that had not been pricked by the hypodermic needle. He was one of the few men who ever managed to quit the king drug. After he shook off the drug habit he alternately worked and drank whiskey. Two weeks ago he indulged in a colossal spree and topped it with overmuch laudanum. Before he had time to recover himself or put up another of his brilliant, laughing fights, his heart was as good as a dead one and the doctors who looked at him shook their heads.

To quote Kid's own use of the vernacular, he had "pied his form." In describing the unpleasant duties incident to the work of a sheriff in a certain wild section of Utah, Kid once said that the sheriff's office was "on the hook." And the blurred story that told Kid's life has been lifted from the hook by the Master Foreman.

Who shall say that mercy will not follow the reading?

A Dead Clown

A dead clown! The words sound odd, don't they? They do not pretend to give a sure-enough picture. They are, in fact, used for an opposite purpose.

Can you imagine a clown's dying? Hardly. All other men are credited with human feelings, with power to love and hate, but one cannot imagine that even death could bring dignity to a clown. For Pierrot must be none other than Pierrot, and can one be quite serious when thinking of the final, agonized twitches of that pitiful, painted face? 'Twas ever so, and it is recorded that men of long ago have laughed naturally when court jesters have died of broken hearts. There be many men who would gravely assist their Maker in taking care of the multitudes of swagger, pretentious fools who bustle on every side, and yet would jeer at the tragedy that befell him who, willingly, had worn the pointed cap and played above the sawdust. A clown dead--a clown suffer? You see the picture as it must be, and it is funnier so. You have already seen him weep, and 'twas his most comical trick. The face was fashioned only for merriment, and death's sweat trickling down his painted lineament would have merely 'roused humor to a shriek of appreciation. No, the mind refuses to permit Pierrot to die or be unmirthful. There are such and such clowns, but a clown in a coffin? The sweet, sweet jest! Even Old Scrooge came at length to laugh and the world approved. Other men have changed from grave to gay, from laughter to tears, and this demeanor is seemly, but to one poor figure the end of lifelong frivolity is a shroud of great, baggy clothes, with fun-paint to distort a ghastly pallor. So the world thinks; clinging to an old world's idea.

    The vision changes, and the humor, for all its certainty, is not free from pathos. Looking back on the centuries one sees the crumbled castles, the cobwebs above decayed biers of emperors, the profound, eternal hush above splendor--sees these with awe, and then remembers, in faint sadness, that even the jesters have died. The stately halls that rise in imagination can do more than give back tomb-like echo. The crown is but dust; and in the far mouldy corner are Pierrot's rotted clothes and bells lying in a dishevelled heap. . . . Seeing a life that has been lived, one is stirred yet again by pleasure that was; mourns, if but slightly, over the sorrow that came; and then recollects, with a sigh, that death has also crept under the old and smaller canvas, and in claiming that dear old painted figure has really stifled the little bright-eyed boy who sat there with his heart attuned to ecstacy and whose eyes found only beauty and peace in the world. Wandering among the things that are dead, man feels regret at every stride--here for mistakes; there for pleasures that have passed; and yet mirth must arise at the clown's sepulchre. Mirth? Aye, mirth always; tears sometimes. So. . . . Pierrot is dead and must die--he and the little child and the perfect sunshine.

The train of thought was suggested by the fate of Leno Wills, the veteran clown, who is now in the county jail serving a thirty-days' term for drunkenness. He was an old-fashioned clown, and one of the best, it is said. He was a star in the ancient one-ring circus, and probably thousands of men and women remember the vast pleasure he brought to their childhood. They would hardly recognize Leno now--such a wreck is he. He is never far from the gutter--when he isn't behind prison bars. Lectures, kindness, moral suasion have no effect. Out of prison in the morning, he is purple-faced at night. The mocking tribute to his former calling is paid by small boys who jeer at him when he is in his cups, and call him by that absurd soubriquet, "Dolly-My-Leg's-Broke." The street scene is familiar: the children crying derisively; the old clown goaded and weeping under the taunts. Homeless, friendless, cheerless, a confirmed dipsomaniac--so the poor old jester nears the end. As he gathers his tatters about him and stands close to the new-made grave, he still must hear the laugh. Only a clown is passing. What matter?

Flashes from the Mire

He came into the restaurant again the other night. He gets more wretched every day. He had a good collegiate education--was a first-honor man, and other men pointed to him and said: "He will do big things." He made one short, brilliant spurt in the world and then fell under the rule of whiskey. That was many years ago. He never rallied, and yet he has not gone to the dogs as other men go. His mind still fights against the grossness of his body, and the bloodshot eyes and the inflamed face are still illumined by an expression of acute intelligence. When he is lowest in debauchery, when his throbbing head falls weakly forward, his lips yet utter high speech, gems of thought from the writers of the classic Addisonian school. He is a creature of the gutter, but his thoughts are not there. His intellect screams under horrid punishment and sparkles brightly above the foulness of its home. Liquor never brings him lethe. The writer has seen him drunk many times, but he was never happily drunk. Unless some miracle be performed, he will die a drunkard. His thirst is maddening, awful--a frightful thing even to witness. His tongue rolls out over parched lips; there is a gulp in the throat, a restless, prowling movement of the body, a hunting, insatiate devil that glows out of the wild eyes. But the whiskey turns on him and makes him a self-mocker, and his brain tortures in its clamor to be allowed to act unhampered. His thoughts are ever on the greater accomplishments--ever in the intellectual realm--for he knows with an aching, weird bitterness that he was rightly destined to deeds of fineness. But he is at the mercy of the curse, and with the last tender quotation from one of the world's masters trembling on his lips, he will die as a dog dies.

Gabriel the Midget

A good many people were interested in the little midget, Gabriel, who did stunts in "A Son of Rest," the production that Mr. Nat Wills presented at the Academy a few nights ago. The little chap made everybody laugh, and seemed very happy while on the stage, but, when viewed closely, it was noticed that there are deep lines on his face and the sorrow of all the ages in his eyes. He is twenty-five years old, and is no larger than a six-year-old boy; and yet he has a man's ideas and a man's intelligence. The sight of a midget makes one shudder. To feel grown up and to have a man's heart and wishes, and then to speak in a thin, piping voice and strut around in No. 1 shoes--ah, it must be awful! No wonder the poor little chap looked sad; and one wonders how the deuce he manages to live at all. He can't do anything to amuse himself. At the hotel the women in the company teased and played with him, and his eyes looked both fierce and sorrowful. May be he is like other men: may be he dreams of holding a soft, delicate head close against his throat; and here the big, frowsy blonde mocks him by patting his head. Little Harold Hooper came up and looked longingly at the midget, with an interrogation point in his eyes. He wanted to invite Gabriel to come out and play with him, and the expression in Gabriel's eyes showed that if Harold made that amiable request he would do his best to slay the first-born of the proprietor of the Central Hotel. Really, a midget must be a keen disappointment to himself. Being a giant is bad enough, because as one potters around he comes across mighty few giantesses who move more gracefully than cows; but being a midget! To have people pity you and look at you as if you were a new kind of fine, red bug--that's the destiny of a midget. Surely the Lord wouldn't hold a little fellow like that responsible for anything he might do. If you were a midget, wouldn't you feel like getting a large pistol and tottering along and shooting somebody just as a mild way of expressing the terrible bitterness that was in your soul!

Wine and Wit

The writer used to know a man who spent most of his life sitting on a dry-goods box and whittling sticks. But about once every three months he would drink an overplus of "corn licker" and quote beautiful, tender things like Browning's "Last Ride." Imagine it, will you?

> "I and my mistress, side by side,
> Shall be together, breathe and ride,
> And, so, one day more am I deified"--

And then another pull at the neck of the bottle that contained the vile, evil-smelling stuff. Yet the sprees were the only thing that made the man interesting. In sober moments he yawned before dinner and discussed the stuff he liked to eat; but with a pint of corn whiskey his voice wore the surging cadence of an impassioned orator, and with a quart he fairly wept over his own eloquence and his exquisite thoughts. He became quite an object of reproach in a church-going place, yet to this day his townspeople bristle with pleasure when he starts on his periodical jaunt to the distillery. This man and the foreman are somewhat alike, though the foreman would not have swallowed the poetry even with the corn liquor as a chaser. Which is a strong way of explaining the foreman's aversion to the pretty gift of song.

A Dandy

You are always at liberty to spot an ass when you travel because you never know how confidently the other man is listening for your own bray. This assertion is by the way. The writer is thinking of a type that he met a few days ago. It was in a railroad waiting room. A young man came in smelling loud of perfumery. He wore new clothes, new shoes, and a new hat that rested on the back of his head and allowed a display of hair that was parted in the middle and fell low on his forehead. His collar was too high and his tie was of purplish hue. He was most affable. He opened a new valise which contained, among other things, a lot of cigarettes, two bottles of whiskey, and a picture with a glass frame. He asked everybody to drink. Nobody drank. He pulled out the picture and said, "That, gentlemen, is the girl I am going to marry." The fattest drummer sighed and looked bored. Nobody said anything. The pasteboard in the picture-frame was decorated with gaudy little red flowers and birds. A brooch at the neck of the girl in the picture shone brilliantly under goldish paint. "That's the finest girl in the land," said the youth, as he carefully laid the photo above the bottles of corn liquor. Along with others in the waiting room he got on the train. He was restless and communicative--roamed all over the train and puffed clumsily at many cigarettes. Finally, at a small station, he picked up his valise and got off. The girl in that picture was there to meet him, and as she shook hands with him he blew cigarette smoke in her face. He looked as if he thought she ought to be awful proud of him. She was proud and pleased, and attempted no concealment. He pulled on a pair of brand new and very yellow gloves, tilted his hat a little further back on his head, blew his nose with a stiff new handkerchief, and strode away--a lion in his home-coming, a laddie who had joined his lassie on that beautiful Christmas morning.

And the fattest drummer fairly snorted.

A Bit of Hayseed

I was on a train between Salisbury and Asheville. The first-class coach was occupied by men only--bored-looking men who rode in silence. When the train stopped at a small station a red-cheeked country girl suddenly appeared in the aisle. She had a smiling face, bright, happy eyes, and wore a muchly washed skirt that was too short, and starchy looking white stockings. She looked down the aisle, courtesied, and said genially: "Good morning."

The man closest to her turned to see the man to whom the girl spoke. He found every man in the car turning to look at the man behind him; and then it dawned on the occupants of the car that the salutation was addressed to everybody in the coach. The silence was not broken. The girl rode fifty miles, then stood up in the aisle once more, looked down the car and said cheerfully:

"Well, good-bye," and left the train.

Again there was silence. Men looked at one another stealthily and smiled. They had had a breath from the sweet green fields--had been touched with kindly hayseed.

John R. Morris

The death of John R. Morris marked the passing of an original man. He knew the other man; knew human nature; saw weakness and strength, and found good in almost everybody. He used to drop in here and sit across the table; and one never knew whether he would discuss the art of the sixteenth century, the weakness of a United States senator, or the poetry of Walt Whitman; but he showed exact knowledge in whatever he talked about. He knew the history of the Booth family, dates and all; laughed at passages in Chaucer; found the discrepancies in Josephus; had intense admiration for St. Paul; could have written a biography of Charles the Fifth; and was very much interested in the boll weevil. And he looked up from some abstruse Hebrew doctrine to say that he liked "John Halifax, Gentleman," more than any book he had ever read. He was in his own class--a genius who loved Ruskin, and sold tin cups. But in him there was no contradiction or inconsistency. He was the odd man who found everything interesting, from a butterfly to a man of war; and yet he stood on his feet and smiled long before he died, in admitting that the hand of death was upon him. And this was the last thing he ever wrote: "Never mind, old friend; there will be a time when we can see better--when seemingly dark and blank areas over our head will bud with tender stars."

Governor Aycock

It is not necessary to add anything to the sketch of Mr. Daniels, and yet the Governor is such an interesting man that one can hardly say enough words about him. I think his curious consistency of character impresses one more than anything else in his make-up. Like the rest of mankind, he has lights and shadows in his life, and a variety of moods, yet underneath all this he has a pleasing sameness that is the essence of reliableness. I have seen him in an old dressing-gown, smoking a short clay pipe; have seen him surrounded by flattering women; have seen him stand within four feet of the President of the United States and make a speech that was admittedly better than the speech of the President; and yet I could see no difference in the Governor or the man. He is a rare being who is absolutely devoid of pretense or affectation, and this is so simply and strongly marked in him that it must immediately impress a stranger or a child. He lacks not in dignity, but any man in the commonwealth can approach the Governor and find the real heart of the man. He has become notable in his own State and abroad, and he must grow greater because he is intensely sincere, intensely earnest, intensely patriotic.

Walter Page

There is nothing to add to this simple tale of a busy, happy life, though much might be said in appreciation. It has been said that Mr. Page is the greatest North Carolinian, and in making a comparison to define his place in the literary world the survey would not be confined to a single continent. It has been said also--and this is by the way--that at times he has criticised with undue severity certain phases of life down here. In this he makes no defense, needs no defense. It is remembered, however, that at the educational meeting in Charlotte last May he spoke, and his theme was North Carolina and the natural bigness of her people. He believes in the State--loves it, and marked it for a glorious future. He did this without the maudlin sentiment that is so common and meaningless. And his criticisms have been, likewise, crisp and clean--honest and kindly.

This writing struggles against the enthusiasm that would so easily come. It is difficult to keep from praising a man who always thinks understandingly and writes without adjectives.

A Professor and His Banjo

The comment man is proud to admit publicly that he has a great fondness for Dr. C. Alphonso Smith, professor of English at the State University, who made an address at Davidson College the other day. Dr.

Smith is one professor who is very much like folks. There may be other professors like this, but they are generally at the bottom of the barrel. Dr. Smith is quite on to his job and can discourse in the genuine Chaucer--the bloomin' chanticleer part and all--but he is not foolish about it. He has a quality of horse-sense that is priceless--and he picks the banjo. No piano, or guitar, or violin, but a banjo that gives out old-fashioned negro melodies and allows an unctuous, unmeaning carol of the cotton field. The fact is noted merely in passing. Dr. Smith has reputation outside of North Carolina and he deserves it. He is a big man in his profession, and he will grow bigger. All the ultraisms that there may be in his craft he has at his tongue's end; and yet it is good to think that he is an artist with the banjo--good to think that students are under the supervision of a man who, however learned he may be, has the heart to turn from the dryness of book lore and knock a banjo silly. Yes, Dr. C. Alphonso Smith is nicely like folks.

Minister Wu

By this time Minister Wu has become settled in his old home in China. Several people were laughing the other day about Mr. Wu's visit to this city. Residents proudly showed him all there was to see of progress and local industrial development; showed him the Mecklenburg monument and took him through cotton mills and other big plants. But what interested the Celestial more than anything he saw during his stay in Charlotte was a made-in-Germany cloth register that he found in the Gingham Mill.

The first time the writer ever saw Minister Wu he was coming down a narrow, befouled street in the old city of Shanghai. He sat in a magnificent Sedan chair. Before him were outriders and footmen shouting strange jargon and carrying big placards which told of their master's official position. The smell about was so strong that it could have been almost cut with a knife, but the minister--he was a mere taotai then--was on his native heath. He is there now, and he is happier there than he was at any State dinner in Washington. Scratch a Chinaman for a thousand years and you will find a--Chinaman. We think we will teach things to those people; they know we will never teach them.

Major Steadman

The Daughters of the Confederacy were fortunate in getting Major Charles M. Steadman, of Greensboro, to make the address at the exercises to be held to-morrow in honor of General Robert E. Lee and General Stone-wall Jackson. Major Steadman may or may not be nominated for the governorship, but he has always been, and will be till he dies, what is much better than being Governor--the best type of a Southern gentleman. The writer offers an apology for this public dealing with Major Steadman's personality; and yet knowledge of him has been public for a good many years. He is one of the older men in this State that the younger men point at with pride, or as a model in manners and for the unfailing consideration that he shows to all with whom he comes in contact. The tribute that he receives now and will receive is worth more than all political honors. He is as clean in ideas and in dress as a refined woman; he has the bow of a Chesterfield; and he gives honest, not assumed, courtesy and deference to men thirty years his junior. In saying that such a type is rare one hazards a drastic criticism, yet the type is rare. Speaking broadly, an old man is not half so thoughtful or sympathetic as an old woman, and he is apt to make too open use of the advantage his years and experience give him. He is less tolerant with youth, and he too often considers it his privilege to drop affability and shroud himself closely in the dignity of his years. He lifts his hat not so often, loses enthusiasm in a hand-shake, and makes one approach him with a respect that precludes confidence. This is written with reverence for age, yet with wonder over one misfortune of age. Lord, what opportunities old men neglect for giving happiness! Youth values so much the appreciation and comradeship of age, and the old men who are kindly and unselfish and pat youth on the back are the best-beloved people in the world. Every man has in mind a few such old men and finds it difficult to understand why all old men are not that way. Respect that they demand could be so quickly had without the asking if they smiled more generously and were less dictatorial and opinionative, and to respect would be added more honor and admiration. A man lives not very long before he discovers that nobody beneath the stars is really wise, and that all speech shows the impress of ignorance, in varying degrees, on human brain. Age could so sweetly afford to be humble in the knowledge it attains. Added years could give so much warmth and encouragement to youth just by a friendly touch, by sympathy; and could add so much to its own high estate in the niceties that govern the smaller as well as the larger affairs of life. It is because Major Steadman thinks of these things that he is held up for inspection. If he wins in the political race it will be not so much because he is a statesman and a Confederate veteran, but because he has given the young men reason to love him. If he loses, they will love him still, for the old man courteous is so rare as to be prized; so complete is the purpose of his making that love and gratefulness will encompass him to the very end.

Rev. George Atkinson

This community misses Rev. George H. Atkinson, who has gone down to Monroe to take charge of the Presbyterian church there. Excepting his boyhood days, he had lived here only a little while, but he managed, without effort, to make everybody like him. And he liked everybody. His life, apart from what he had to say in the pulpit, was a daily ministry. Always he shook hands with people and smiled joyously; always he was sympathetic and had kind words to say. He did not talk religion overmuch, but he showed the world that his religion had made him perfectly happy and had stimulated his sense of humor. He was equally at home with the mill operative and the patrician, and he was loved by both because he lived the doctrine of unselfishness and radiated love as he breathed. He generally made people think better of themselves, and thus he exercised fine, gentle art, unflavored by flattery. He never jarred or rubbed the wrong way, for his tact was part of his religion. He was not a man who made big impressions, for his influence was subtle, though insistent--the quality of a man who would offer strength to help weakness, gladness to bless happiness, or intuitive sympathy as heartsease. He is not a man to rave over, and this is not raving. 'Tis the honest appreciation that does not usually come to a man until after he is dead. George Atkinson may not be a great preacher, but he does good just by living and touching his fellow man. The man who would go out of his way to say one kindly thing to another man is to be counted an exception. George Atkinson wishes to help all mankind by gentle speech. If he were to die to-morrow his life might be termed perfect in its purpose and use of opportunities; and the largeness of his simple living must constitute the apology for this thrust at his privacy.

The Last of the Romans

The last of the Romans says few words to any man, and he is seen oftenest as he bends his whited head and waters his roses. He has finished with the long fray--has seen all there is to see in life; and now, in the evening, he leaves the haunts of men and leans tenderly over the smallest rosebud that blossoms in the tangled hedge. He is the most striking figure that comes on these streets; and he walks alone and unheeding save when he is stopped now and then by one who would ask a kindness. He, who has seen all his generation pass into dust, has found solitude without courting it, but since it has come he takes it as a philosopher unafraid--clear-eyed, strong, straight, not stooping except where the roses grow. If he has always cared for flowers that is not known. He has been in the great, tumultuous struggles and has done his part therein. Maybe he had no time for flowers then, but he loves them now, and makes them supreme in the interest of his living. They keep the last of the Romans from being too severe; and he is very human and approachable as he--distinguished jurist and gentleman--stands by the rose bush, still touched with the glories of the dying sun.

CHAPTER IV
NEGRO TYPES

Little Hinry

Little Hinry has been exiled.

Black as ebony he is and only twelve years of age; and because one leg came under a railroad car Hinry must forever bob along upon a cheap, wooden thing that may not be called a leg even in mockery.

But Hinry has incurred the displeasure of the recorder and Hinry is banished from the streets.

Everybody knows Hinry--knows that shrewd, impish grin and remembers that--

"Shine, sir? Shine?" For Hinry is, or was, a boot-black, privileged to shine shoes without paying the usual license. He found an old dry goods box and he rigged up an old chair which was the joy and pride of his life; and Hinry plied his trade and kept hunger from his small body.

But the recorder laid his heavy, just hand on Hinry and Hinry is exiled.

Aye, but the crime of Hinry was grievous--enough to tax the patience of the recorder. Hinry quarrelled with two other little boys who teased him, and because he hobbled around and gathered stones and made as if to throw these at his tormentors, he was arrested by the stalwart officers of the law and was accorded the honor of a trial in the open and honorable court.

Because the offense was so great, it was meet that the punishment should be great, and so it is eminently right that Hinry should go into exile-- this Hinry who has trampled underfoot--only one foot--the law of his native land.

For four years Hinry, who has a grandmother and a comfortable bed, has never sought his home save when the weather was bitter and he could not stay out of doors. When the elements have been kind Hinry has slept, by preference, in alley-ways, dry-goods boxes, and very often in The Observer building. He had the run of the place here, and many a time and oft he has climbed on the window ledge in the front office of the print shop and has composed himself to slumber in plain view of many policemen. When aroused he growled and grinned and consented to move not further away from his improvised couch than the carpeted corridor that leads to the editorial rooms of this paper. Here Hinry has slept countless times, curled up like a little, black, maimed dog.

But Hinry, who has so cruelly broken the law and is an exile, will sleep here no more.

The poor, old, worn-out chair, which glorified the life of little Hinry, has gone--banished also by the just edict of Recorder Shannonhouse. For very many days the chair has stood just in front of The Observer building, and little Hinry tried to entice into its embrace all manner of men. They will not be molested now--these customers of little Hinry--this little black waif who must needs wander on deserted back streets and weep in memory of a happiness that is lost.

For the recorder was firm, as he should have been, and gave orders to the police that if ever Hinry is seen on the streets again he must be arrested. And Hinry's arrest, be it known, will mean summary conviction and imprisonment on the chain-gang.

And so one more foul disturber of the peace has suffered a well-merited fate, and yet again the recorder can sleep in the perfect assurance of duty well performed.

Hinry--little black Hinry--will no longer threaten the welfare of this community.

For Hinry is an exile.

The Coon-dog Ceremony

By 9:30 yesterday morning a large number of visiting and resident Masons and other interested spectators had gathered in the large auditorium at the park to witness the performance of the famous coon-dog marriage ceremony by its author, Col. D. G. Maxwell. Publication had been made merely as to the fact that the negro couple would be married, and as to the exact mode or form of the nuptials speculation was rife.

The preparations for the ceremony were ridiculous beyond words. Wearing the robe of Cardinal Richelieu, borrowed from the Peters & King Stock Company, and false wig, moustache and beard, Colonel Maxwell advanced to the centre of the stage, followed by five or six nobles. One of these was Mr. A. E. Fugle, of Columbia, S. C., who carried a shot gun at present arms, while Mr. R. W. Roberts waved a sabre. The other nobles were Messrs. C. P. Snuggs, W. J. King and C. E. Stenerson.

At a signal, Mr. Robert Ogden, who was seated at the piano, began the wedding march, "The Georgia Camp Meeting." Entering through the main door, the bridal couple, Ephraim Johnson and Margaret Williams, came down the centre aisle, preceded by Sam Mosely, who held aloft a huge bouquet. With his arm round his bride, the groom advanced the full length of the hall at cake-walk pace. To make the affair more absurd, both were quite solemn.

After a moment's wait in the dressing-room the bridal couple marched on the stage to slow music. Then came the sonorous voice of Colonel Maxwell in the words of his own invention.

"We have assembled here together, my friends and brother Masons, upon this historic spot," said he, "to celebrate the nuptial ties of the couple now present. And as they launch their boat off in the ocean of connubial bliss, we will bid them 'olive oil' and fling an old shoe and a handful of rice forninst them; and may their hull be free from the barnacles of life, and be never subject to squalls, nor cries of 'ship ahoy!' " Here the Colonel asked the usual questions required by law, and then, in stentorian voice, pronounced the couple man and wife, "by the authority vested in him by the Commonwealth of North Carolina, which is sometimes called the Tar Heel State of this confederation of fusion, and by the county of Mecklenburg, known as the cradle of American liberty; by the smoking tar kilns and the bleeding sentinels of our turpentine fields; by the old flea-bitten coon dog, whose basso-profundo voice is heard in the gloaming; by recollections of the fat baked opossum, with sides lined with sop, sweet potatoes and hoe-cake, to say nothing of the sweet and luscious 'watermillion'; by the free-silver fake of 16 to 1, which some think is the panacea of all national ills; by the Dingley tariff-bill, which is to bring forth the long-wished-for wave of prosperity; by the song of the gold-bug, which some say is the dirge of the people and the glorification of trusts and monopolies; by the loud and clarion notes of the old Shanghai chanticleer, heard in the early morn calling upon his comrades to shake off their lethargy; and last, but not least, by the memory of the Decklenburg Mecklapendence of Injuration. Whomsoever the laws of North Carolina have joined together, let no man put asunder. Salute your bride, and may the Lord have mercy upon your souls!"

The utter absurdity of the situation convulsed the entire audience with laughter. The bridal couple smiled appreciatively, just as star-actors. Evidently they had rehearsed to some effect, for at the conclusion of the ceremony the nimble groom, garbed in a long frock coat and carrying a frayed silk hat in his hand, sprang to the centre of the stage and faced his bride, who was arrayed in white lawn over black, and who began to quickstep with body thrown far back in cake-walk style. Their dancing was superb. 'Twas too utterly ridiculous to be true; and the audience applauded in screams. Again and yet again the dusky couple were encored, and twice they returned to the stage to introduce some novelty in step-dancing. Finally they left the stage and proceeded, in cake-walk dance, through the auditorium and into the open. A few minutes previous to their departure, their attendant, Sam Mosely, passed a silk hat among the audience and collected money sufficient to defray the expenses of a wedding trip. Thus was the coon-dog ceremony performed.

Aunt Cynthia

The funeral services of "Aunt" Cynthia Carson were conducted at the residence of Mr. and Mrs. James H. Carson, on South Tryon street, at 3:30 o'clock yesterday afternoon, by Rev. Dr. J. R. Howerton, pastor of the First Presbyterian Church. The pall-bearers, all well-known colored men, were Moses Shipp, Noah French, Willis Brice, and Love Williams.

Many flowers were there, the testimony of affection of members of the Carson family and many others. Conspicuous in the floral offerings was a calla lily cross sent by Mrs. Harvey H. Orr.

The services were simple, yet impressive. Aunt Cynthia lived in a house in the rear of the Carson home. From here the body was carried to the Carson residence and placed in the parlor. Practically all the Carson family and connection and other white people, together with a score or more of the older colored persons, assembled in the large rooms to pay the last tribute to the aged woman.

The hymns, "How Firm a Foundation" and "Asleep in Jesus," were sung, and Dr. Howerton made a brief, earnest address, touching on the good qualities of "Aunt" Cynthia and holding up her life as a memorial to faithfulness and love.

The Carson family and others, including the negroes, followed the body to Pinewood Cemetery.

The funeral services presented a Southern picture in full simplicity and beauty. A mammy of the old type had passed. She rested in state for a time in the big house, to use the negro vernacular, and this rounded up honorably a life that was humbly perfect.

"Aunt" Cynthia was nearly ninety years old. She had been a slave of the Carson family before the war, and she had served Mr. and Mrs. James H. Carson for half a century. She nursed every one of their children and held them as her own children. From the parents and from the children she demanded and received a common share in happiness and sorrow. All that touched the family touched her. Her whole life was one of service and loyalty.

She knew not a great deal that happened outside her people, and cared to know but little. The Carson boys were her boys and remained her boys until she died. She watched over them unceasingly when they were small, and when they became grown she still claimed a part in their lives. She did not lose her early idea of her slavery, but it was a pretty idea that carried dignity without undue obeisance.

When the old black mammy became too old for service, Mr. James H. Carson built her a house in the rear of his own residence and there she spent her last days in peace. Every Sunday afternoon each one of the Carson men visited her. They came to her, too, at other times, and their wives and children gave to her the affection that was so readily returned. She kept up with what every member of the family was doing and was privileged to ask any question she pleased. She was the best type of her race, and her living and its meaning stand for an ideal that will live as the South will live.

Such deaths in the South have become rare. Ten years from now they will not occur. The aged negro who was both servant and friend of the white man is seen infrequently. The type shows a certain grandeur for all its lack of ostentation. Three years ago, when Col. W. R. Myers, of this city, lay on his death-bed, an old ex-slave came unsummoned and sat by his master until his master and friend had died. No one was surprised, yet future generations must uncover in memory of such a scene.

"Aunt" Cynthia's vision was confined to the big house and her own little dwelling, and her life's purpose was single, clear and very beautiful. In her own mind and heart she found the perfect reward here. In her last days she had her own servant to nurse and tend her, and her condition brought many anxious, sympathetic faces to her bedside. The old black mammy had failed in nothing and had given all she had to give of love; and the blessed consummation of her devotion came when love was leaning over and touching her even as the spirit went out.

Major Jim Fox

Old Major Jim Fox is dead and buried. Don't you remember him? Then you know nothing of life in the Central Hotel as it was fifteen years ago. Major Fox was employed in the office and he was always at the front. He was but little taller than his feet were long, and he had hands fit to shake with a bear. He was a Mecklenburg product, and was gray-haired when he first entered the employment of Eccles & Bryan, thirty-five years ago. He was somewhere in the nineties. Perhaps he was a hundred. Who knows?

As a hotel attaché, Major Fox was strictly attentive to business. No guest ever laid down a half-consumed cigar and picked it up again--not while the major was on duty. Both Mr. Bryan and Mr. Eccles had that habit, but he broke them of it so effectually that they have never returned to it, although old Jim has not been about them for years. Then, as a tip-taker he was an artist. An old patron of the Central said that the major always got him for a dime as soon as he landed from the 'bus and handed over his grip; got him for another dime when shown to his room; got him for another dime when he came shuffling in with ice water, and was sure to tap him at every contact during his stay at the hotel. "And do you believe it," he continued, "after I was in the 'bus and ready to go to the depot, it somehow seemed that the 'bus would not leave until old Jim had held me up for a final dime."

The major's salary as head porter of the Central was not as big as that of the ordinary bank president, yet the old darkey became rich, in a way, and bought up good real estate. At the height of his prosperity he was induced by two Central Hotel darkies to chip in and run an excursion to Wilmington. It was a success, and the three partners made what each considered a pile of money. Then Major Fox, although the watermelon season had passed, conceived the idea of running an excursion of his own. He chartered a train of six cars on the Southern for an excursion from Charlotte to Winston. On the morning his train was to leave, six passengers applied for tickets. Major Fox was sure of getting 20 at Harrisburg, 100 at Concord, 30 at China Grove, 50 at Salisbury, 10 at Lexington, and 200 at Greensboro. Those were his figures, and despite the entreaties of his friends to abandon his project, he hurriedly secured a lawyer, gave a mortgage on his property, borrowed $265 on it, paid it over to the Southern agent, and took out his excursion train. The train was run to Winston according to contract, but barring the major and the six passengers with which he started from Charlotte, it reached Winston empty. The old man never recovered from the blow, but he was cured of running excursions. He gave up his job at the hotel and thenceforth had hard lines to the end.

Poor old Jim! What a shower of tips he would get if that capacious black hand could be stretched out in the flesh to-day to those who were wont to keep it polished in times gone by.

The Color Line

In this country a child draws the color line early, as by an instinct. Now, young Neil Pharr, Junior, the son of State Senator Neill Pharr, is a wee bit of a boy only about four years old, and God and his people have been kind in giving to him Elsie, a black mammy, who loves him with a tenderness and fierceness that are beautiful. She gives to him perfect devotion, devotes to him all her life. They are comrades by night and in day they are ever together--this aged motherly woman with the cheery face and the bright little boy in his first trousers. In the family deliberations it has been permitted the black mammy--white-hearted as a princess of the blood--to sit in the intimate semi-circle that faces the fire at eventide. Young Neill has reached the age that takes notice of life about. A little while ago, as his mammy sat there, big, comfy and at ease, he walked to her and, taking her hand, silently led her to a chair a few feet in the rear of the family circle. "You, mammy," he said, with no lack of tenderness in his voice--"You, mammy, sit here." He walked back to the circle and, resuming his seat by his father, gazed thoughtfully into the fire. There was a moment's silence and everybody looked at either the black mammy or her boy. Then a voice from the chair Further Back came trembling with delight and saying:

"Marse Neill--oh, Marse Neill, ain't he pure white?"

Here's the kindliest solution of the race question. Here are the love, the loyalty and the appreciation; but the negro must sit back--Further Back. And the negro, the best negro, laughs and understands.

A Faithful Slave

Only a few months ago a Southern gentleman, aged past the allotted span, came to die in this city. Without the asking there came from Texas a negro, a former slave, who was of his master's age. Through weeks of a lingering illness he sat by the side of his old master. He nursed him as one would tend a beloved brother. And he was the faithful, watchful servant until death had closed his master's eyes. At the last touch of analysis, you will find that the thing that made the old negro come back to his dying master formed the basis of the present well-being of the negro. As the old servant, he is loved for that; for that his son is liked and his education is welcomed. The feeling is a blind, indefinable something that includes the bootblack and the bishop, and holds one as far from equality as the other. This knowledge is the birthright of a Southern child and is imbibed by all who come South to live. It is fair, accurate and unchangeable, and it is the soul of harmony.

Mother and Child

Frequently one sees in the streets here a little colored girl about three years old. She is bow-legged to a remarkable extent; she is very black with not a pleasing facial contour; and, moreover, she is petulant and ill-tempered. Yet her mother, who always accompanies her, dresses the child as if she were the heiress of thousands and had the grace of a wood nymph. She wears a bit of a gold bracelet on her arm, and her distorted figure is clothed in clinging white things that might become a tiny princess. She and her mother slowly walk the length of the streets--past beautiful children with eyes of blue and brown, and the woman's croon and the look on her face tell that she finds no greater love than her own--no more perfect child than the dusky toddler at her side. Yet there is nothing wonderful in the picture. It is but a quaintly pitiful illustration of the great mother-love that refuses to see blemish and blesses the world.

"Misery"

It is to be hoped that no amount of education will prevent the negroes from using certain words that are peculiarly their own. Was there ever a time that the colored people failed to misuse the word "misery;" could any word be more expressive? Your old colored mammy tells you that she has a misery in her side, and you know that she has used the only suitable word. A negro woman, smartly dressed, went into a drug store last night and complained of a misery in her head, and her eyes showed the feeling. "Misery" is really the best descriptive word for some purely physical emotions. Misery in the head! No other word can be half so expressive, or serve as a synonym. . . . Misery! You see the figure bowed in the dark and the long-shuddering ache--the pain that means utter exhaustion. . . . There is the faint smell of medicine, the weary tossing on pillows--the intense, quick loudness of little outer noise. And there is other misery in the head--this vital, indefinable force that offers black pictures to the gaze of insomnia, or cries for remembrance of evil things, or grips taut nerves as a summons for Remorse to come to the white night.

CHAPTER V
WOMAN AND HER WORLD

Mirrors

The subject came up the other night:

Are mirrors deceptive? And it is so. You look in one glass and you have that creamy complexion, that dreamy, soft look in your eyes, and fine curving lines; but another mirror, on the same day, shows you to be liverish-visaged, be-grinned consciously and unattractively, and wrinkled beyond your ears and years.

In two separate houses in this place there are glasses of the before-and-after-taking species. One, kind with a lie, allows a woman to go out with lack-lustre eyes and plebeian mould, pleased in her heart with the beauty that only the mirror tells. The other glass basely mocks Miss Dainty Face--mocks Dainty Face in trying lights and shadows. Did not the world deny the tale and wage warfare on the mirror unhappiness might come. . . . But the great secret is not to be told by mirrors after all. The quality of fascination--the thing that holds without wish for release--that is not as the virtue of the clean-limbed, perfect-faced. 'Tis the clear, sweet, hidden touch of a soul--the essence, indefinable, of intense, shuddering longing; the epitome of all peace. With a high head raised for choice, man sometimes looks admiringly at the perfect woman, svelte, clear-eyed, patrician, warm and cold . . . and loves past heartsease the frailest invalid that ever misery made selfish. No; mirrors . . . nor nothing . . . can tell.

Too Knowing

"I've no use for these men who know things about a woman's clothes," said a Charlotte lady the other day. "A married man ought to know the instant his wife or his daughter needs a new dress or hat, but an unmarried man has no business knowing the difference between an old gown and a new gown, and he shouldn't know, for instance, that there is such a thing in the world as a silk lining. Nothing gives me the creeps so quickly as the feeling that I am being sized up by a man. There are two or three of these effeminate critical men in Charlotte and all the women resent their covert inspection. A woman dresses at and for other women, and a man's criticism is a cruel stab from an unexpected quarter. Why, I lost liking for one of the best friends I ever had simply because in a thoughtless moment he told me how many evening dresses I had and described each one of them. The only way I could have punished him properly would have been to marry him, but the price of revenge was too dear--and, besides, he said that the thought of a woman in a kimona bored him to death. That was the limit. So long as a woman isn't slouchy, or doesn't try to produce an effect with an assortment of colors that would jar a mule, she ought to be free from a male expression of opinion as to the quality of her clothes."

The Tactless Woman

"I've been talking to a tactless woman," said the observant resident, "and I feel kind of sick. Oh, it doesn't make any difference about a man. A man's a clumsy thing in finer matters, and you are not surprised when he stumbles and says the wrong thing. But Nature must laugh mockingly every time a tactless woman is born. Ugh! It is awful. You see, you can't take a club--of course you can't. You couldn't make any impression that way. Here's a creature that is so delicately and finely constituted from birth that she ought to be able to lift her head up and know by instinct what to say and do under all circumstances. Because of this assumption, she is allowed all privileges. She may discuss any subjects, however sacred; and nine times out of ten she is the soul of tact in dealing with a situation that involves any kind of feeling. When she is an exception to this rule, she is an unnatural something, a freak, an unmeaning torturer who strolls around and jerks at tense, quivering nerve. 'To know how to do'--that's a term that means more in the world of women than in the world of men. Not a great deal is expected of a man. If he keeps his face and linen clean and throws his shoulders back and doesn't talk too much, that is enough. He may have a great many or very few parlor tricks and graces, but they are not essential. If he is easy in his manner and doesn't put to shame the woman who is with him, he'll get along all right. In other words, a man doesn't have to know how to do very much, and he can continually learn how to rub off the rough places and improve himself. But it is different with a woman. There is no hope for a tactless woman--the most maimed thing in life. She causes more suffering than the toothache, and a worse kind of suffering. She hasn't a bad heart; she means well, and she goes into the innermost places and just hops around on the tenderest corns. She is a travesty on her sex and is to be pitied. In her general demeanor she is like one who stabs you under a flag of truce; for the tactless woman will go anywhere and dare to do anything. Her ailment is incurable and is spotted at a glance. To be more correct, one feels her--feels the jar of her presence, whether she be active or inactive. Carelessly, unknowingly, she goes along making sores and trampling on sore places. She is never rebuked; one never quarrels with the tactless woman. One may not cry out against the hurt that she inflicts. She causes the world to wince in pain, but all her victims are silent. And she is everywhere--poor, miserable blunderer.

The Flirt

Every now and then there wanders into the village a young woman who has achieved a reputation as a scalp-taker, and who proceeds to play a little game of hearts with the local swains. The result is usually harmless, for the woman who has the misfortune to be advertised as a professional flirt, has not, as a rule, qualities that will make a lasting impression on a man. Nine times out of ten the woman who is publicly marked dangerous is not dangerous--except, possibly, to small boys. The women who belong to the class that may provoke a revolution or send men to the devil may be flirts, but the world never thinks to classify them as such. In other words, real fascination is a low-voiced, quiet-moving thing and travels unheralded; and the name of the woman who inspires love or does deep hurt is not apt to be flaunted.

Flirting is the outcome of civilization and a sign of sexual equality. Our ancestors--good old pirates--flirted only with clubs, and it is only in the last few centuries that their female descendants have been accorded the privileges of polite dalliance and a parade of captives in dress clothes.

Flirting is a game that is played with brains and without brains, and lacking brains it is as the taste of heavy, stale beer. It may be perfection in eyes, hair, form and clothes, but unbacked by mental smoothness or finesse it is a stupid and a wearisome thing. When two fools play the game the gods must laugh, for nothing is more ludicrous than a bold tongue's clumsy movement in flattery or love-making.

Is the pastime to be condemned altogether? Of course. It too often carries the curse of cheapening the man and the woman, or it may cause needless heartaches and remorse. Yet it is a social habit that does not weaken under censure. We may hold up Priscilla, the Puritan maiden, who voiced sincerity and only that; but yonder is the tilted-chinned daughter of the Cavalier, with a half-challenging, heavy look in her eyes. And for her hypocritical, constant, tender, imperious, wilful, gentle, mocking, serious self the world will forgive much.

A Man's Point of View

And there is the girl who wishes all men to like her, and no man really likes that sort of girl. She always looks through him for the next man, and hasn't time to pause and cultivate one good friend. The girl who makes an open bid for popularity and likes anything in a man's clothes had better marry quick to save neglect. Men are shy at heart with a woman who looks alike at all men, but they will gladly tie to the kind that has common sense and naturalness enough to discriminate. The girl who finds unhappiness at the end of a campaign for general admiration gets an inevitable result and no sympathy. She is a common blunderer and too often seen. My lady who is kind-hearted and very particular wears well and longest.

"And there's the kind of a woman that a man wants to marry," continued the observant man. "She may not be beautiful, or clever, or particularly good, but she is the sort of person that he would like to be his wife. The man may not propose to her, or be in love with her, but mentally, at least, he stamps her for wifehood, and long, sweet wear. It is providential that all men do not think alike on this subject; but every man has selected his own class--has decided as to what woman he thinks he, or any other man, ought to be proud to marry. A man may not discuss such things, for his judgment praises a few women and is not complimentary to the majority. Any man, saving a fool, knows that most women are far too good for him, but, being a mere man, he seeks for the Princess when he comes to wed. He finds her according to his taste, and she may be outside the sacred class that his mind has designated; but his ideals are unshattered, and he will go on through life marking those who would bless as wife and those who wouldn't.

"The thing is as natural as breathing. Every man who knows women is continually making the secret dividing line, and every time he talks to a woman he is prepared to tell if she belongs to, or is excluded from, his list of women-for-wives.

"And a woman? A woman knows quicker than a man--knows at a glance. Because she is a finer thing her class is stricter as to entries. Sometimes she dies after wifehood and motherhood . . . and there have been no entries."

An Enigma

But women are more contradictory than men, and, therefore, more interesting. The few women who are even-tempered and steady-going are the ones you would like to tie to, but life is made tumultuous and attractive by the women who may be commonplace or æsthetic, or sunshine and tempest, all in the space of five minutes. Most of the celebrated women in history had an impartial fondness for murder and babies; and in every-day life one remembers longest the woman who is capable of doing anything, and is always doing the thing unexpected. Her variableness is a rare torture and delight. She has a figurative range from pig's feet to cream puffs, and she may be a big, mannish somebody with a square jaw who weeps on your shoulder without provocation, or you observe that she is soft and tiny and ethereal and as black-hearted and treacherous as the worst of the Circes. When you have ceased to be surprised at anything she does you have learned something by experience. When she belongs to you, by any sort of right, you are blessed if you occasionally know what she is for one hour, without caring a baubee what she may be the next hour.

The New Woman

In yesterday's Observer it was perceived that Mr. H. E. C. Bryant ventured to protest against women drinking in public. Mr. Bryant was wrong, of course. Women have a perfect right to drink and smoke in public places. That is part of crying away from thralldom--a glorious part of emancipation. Women drink in New York and in other large cities, and in a cosmopolitan life it is almost universally conceded that they are privileged to smoke. Why should man alone be considered entitled to the perfumery of a brandy and soda or an evil-scented Turkish cigarette? Out on your narrowness, Mr. Bryant! Your staid old North Carolina sentiment is a jangling note. We are behind the times; that is all. We have not yet reached the stage when we concede that a woman shall of right be other than womanly, refined--a dainty, wholesome creature in a background of softness and reserve. Thus we are insular, indeed. And we shall be hidebound in prejudice, it is feared. For, with a Scotchman's yielding stubbornness, the woman's right to drink and smoke may be granted--yes, not cheerily or admiringly, but with condemnation that can be no more courteous than to find concealment in a careless, contemptuous smile. Let the women drink and smoke, Mr. Bryant; and then turn away from them and thank God if you know women who have clean breath and clear eyes.

A Coarse Husband

"He is the kind of a man who tells dirty jokes to his wife," said the observant resident, "and he belongs to a type that every one knows. It is rather odd that a man should marry a young woman, and then try to tarnish her by the unnecessary relation of evil things, but such accomplishment, according to the estimate of some men, is one of the good uses of matrimony. There are a great many men who make a point of telling their wives the stories that unmarried men tell each other in a whisper, and thus the wife becomes a receptacle for knowledge that strikes at her fineness, and is the victim of an intimacy that is neither sacred nor honorable. One doesn't live long before he discovers that women are apt to find out pretty much everything there is to know; but no woman who is worth while can feel pleased, or interested, or amused when her husband seeks to inject humor into the household in the form of a dirty joke. How a man shall comport himself toward his wife is a man's own affair; yet society everywhere is tainted by the foul tales the men carry from the street to the ears of their wives."

The Art of Kissing

Three college magazines that came to this office recently contained love stories, in which all the heroes, in climax, asked the heroines if they wouldn't kiss 'em, please. And, of course, they did. The thing brings to mind a discussion in this town last week as to whether it is usual or proper for a man to ask the interesting psychological question, or whether it is seemly to just proceed. The concensus of opinion seemed to be that a man ought to have sense enough, at a certain juncture, to take action without embarrassing a friend with a useless question. There is a poem about a Danish youth who told a girl that he wished he had a magic whistle that he had heard about; and if he had it he would blow a time or two and then she would let him kiss her. She demurely replied, in effect, that he would be foolish to whistle for what he might take without wasting breath. That's the idea. You can go ahead--or you can't go ahead. But most times when you name it you can't have it.

The Art of Wearing Flowers

What a wealth of chrysanthemums there are here now, and how perfectly natural it is that everybody should like different flowers in a different way. You admire chrysanthemums as you admire a large, well-dressed, showy sort of woman who has a lot of savoir faire and yet is not specially interesting. Chrysanthemums are too masculine; and they can be made to look apoplectic and ashamed by the side of a white carnation. Women ought to be very careful about the kind of flowers they wear. Some women ought not to be allowed to wear violets. They desecrate the tender, tremulous things. American Beauty roses ought to be jammed into a centrepiece and kept there. They are too sensuous for a refined woman to wear. Such coloring is too pronounced in the essence of Buddha's heaven. But, seriously speaking, if you watch flowers and eyes, you will often find lack of harmony. You can't explain; but you will feel the jar. Flowers rebuke moods, too; and temper or fretfulness is reproached by the rosebud below the mutinous lips. One woman in a hundred knows how to wear flowers. Flowers are just tacked on to the rest. The average woman has an occasional right to wear any sort of a flower, but she ought to pray earnestly when she pins violets to her dress. For violets are quite human, you know. Somewhere or other there's a land of quiet, restful beauty where the laugh of a child is the harshest note of joy and where violets, forever clean and wet with the dew-mist, rustle softly in the eternal breath of peace--purity.

The Art of Giving Presents

A man who is a sensible man was bothered over selecting a present to send a young woman, and many men got together and discussed the right thing to do. Opinions varied. Some said jewellery, but that is too dangerous and delicate a matter to argue about. Others said books, and books are always safe and cheap. It is singular, however, that the woman who is certain to appreciate most highly your gift of a book is exactly the kind of a person to whom you would like to give a house and lot. As a rule, books make the greatest hit with your aged relatives, with people who are not literary, or with one particular woman who reads you between the lines. Most discussions about presents to a woman end by trying to decide whether she would prefer candy or flowers. Every woman likes candy, but the woman who prefers flowers to candy--and violets to American Beauty roses--is apt to be the same curious woman who will set more store by a book than a diamond brooch. The woman to whom anything may be given, in utter safety, is the woman who picks up a flower and presses it and keeps it forever. The most intimate possessions of the most womanly woman show that she is altogether crazy and perfectly delicious.

The Mystery of Love

Recently things have happened here that make one speculate about the quality of human love. You may have observed that things like that happen frequently. In truth, we are always being placed in the position of level-headed onlookers who wonder why one person loves, or doesn't love, another person. And generally amazement is caused by the love that continues to love.

In a lifetime each man and each woman understands how and why any man could love a dozen women, but one man and all women cannot understand how or why any woman can love but one man. If it is The Other Man, all men are curious and puzzled, while the other women are sympathetic and puzzled. This is a way of saying that it is much easier to love a woman than to love a man; and in a love affair in which you yourself are not involved, you are given opportunity to be mystified.

Some months ago this paper reprinted a smartly written article that described in detail the causes that inspired love. It was absurd, of course. The enumeration of good qualities and the lordly count of attributes come after the loving, which, unguided by choice, may be based on the nice discrimination of a fool. If one had a chance to vivisect the smooth, undisturbed loves that send to church, build up homes and caress gray hairs, he would find that in their deepest strength these are reasonless and that after all there is not a great deal of difference between these and the love that is held up to the public gaze because it lives, with a glad sigh, after betrayal. Before a man is old he finds that any love that is really worth while is self-sufficient and will live beyond faithlessness, and then he goes out and has his say in the chattering world which discusses the wisdom or unwisdom of the failing.

The greatest blessing that can be given a man or a woman is a love that will live always. If there be requital in kind, then two people are to be numbered among the elect, but the falseness of the one brings the worst misery if it causes the love of the other to die.

There was a woman here and she sat by the side of a man day after day, and the love-light in her eyes never faltered, though the world looked at her and said she was foolish because the man had been unfaithful. People said, "How can she still care?" or "She should leave him!" but the woman smiled and softly touched the man again. What she really thinks no one knows; what she feels thousands saw, and thousands said she was unwise in not ceasing to care. The woman was right for two odd reasons. She could not have stopped loving the man if she had wanted to; and if she could have lost her love, what on earth would she have had left? She gave everything and received nothing, but that was her happiness. There was exaltation in her love. It stood alone, a bright, beautiful thing, supporting her, intensifying her courage. She fed on it eagerly and it never failed to sustain her. It was in the tremulous movement of her hands, in the droop of an eyelid; it was the mainstay of her existence. Suppose she had been robbed of this. Why, if that love had weakened or lessened she would have been infinitely more miserable than she was over all the terror and the heartache and the cruel tales. To have love to die on one's hand, to have ardor give way to weariness, to recognize the first touch of distaste, to feel the slower rushing of the blood--ah, 'tis a curse!

The world said, ungallantly, that the woman was a fool, while the woman continued to twist her hands in her lap and showed in her eyes that she had God's priceless gift.

People shudder over a passion that is misplaced, or speak contemptuously of a love that exists beyond its reward, but such feeling is the one human emotion that deifies, and the real pity must go to the love that is checked by reason, or time, or any circumstance this side the grave. If one loves hopelessly, he is forever blessed if he loves in the full strength of that term.

And the woman, if she had been the lowliest and in tatters, was glorified. She was to be envied. In its holding of happiness, life is, at the last analysis, a one-man or a one-woman proposition, and if God had bestowed on us a feeling such as the woman has He is good even if He points it at a dog, or a man-thing that reeks in the gutter, or a woman-thing that speaks to shame her sex.

If Mrs. Burdick had been a character in a book she would have clenched her hands and perjured her soul, if need be, in her determination to protect as far as possible, at least, one of the two men. Her attitude was in strange contrast to the testimony of a young woman in this State who was the principal personage in a murder trial that occurred some years ago. She had suffered more than any one else and had reason to be vengeful toward one man who was intimately connected with the homicide. But when questioned about this man she said simply, "I love him now better than I love my God." The statement was not essential in her evidence and could have no effect on the verdict of the jury, and yet placed a wrecked life on a high plane. The woman made no excuse for what she had done, but in the presence of the man who had betrayed her and cared nothing for her, she lifted up a dead white face and dignified forever her own ruin. In the public mind she became at once the sacrificial and best element in the tragedy, and her conduct was at once forgivable to a world which was not permitted to show its forgiveness.

Where naked tragedies are seen, or where the large human passions come into play, one is curiously shocked by a display of a weakness that spells littleness. In a consideration of such matters there is in us a thing that will make us look understandingly and leniently upon any emotion that is big, brave, and daring, no matter how bad it is. This is a primeval instinct, which has fineness enough to abhor anything that crawls or stammers or shows fight in the face of a situation that is made or controlled by the supreme workings of love or hate.

It is rather odd that a woman should be content to live forever with a thing like a man, isn't it? As one grows older, he knows that such living is the chiefest blessing, but he is forced to conclude, without being sceptical or unfair, that the woman gives more than the man. 'Tis an old theme; and yet if you walk to the square and stand ten minutes, you will see a woman who is not properly appreciated by a man. The injustice has so thrived that it has become natural, or seems natural, and yet the every-day fresh evidence of it kind of hurts, somehow. Women--the oldest women--retain girlishness, and men forget this--forget, in their ambition or business cares, that women do not lose sentiment or dainty fineness or wish for notice of little bits of feminine things. There is a man and he kisses his wife's hand and still admires her feet, and she is over seventy and as happy as a queen.

Hopeless Resignation

The woman and the child and the man climbed on the street car. The woman had a heavily lined face and looked as if she had suffered so much that she had gotten used to it. She was very thin and tired-looking, but her dress was clean and neat. The child, a little girl, also wore a dress that was fresh and dainty, for all its cheapness. The man's clothes had seen better days, but they were well patched and darned--looked as if a deft-fingered woman was continually bothering over them. The man's nose was red and his eyes were watery. His mouth was very weak. He seemed restless, and crossed and uncrossed his legs. The conductor came and stopped in front of the man. The man looked at the woman and kept his hands in his pockets. The woman opened her purse and after close search produced a quarter. The conductor took the silver and held out ten cents. Hurriedly the man reached out and grabbed the dime. His watery eyes glistened. He turned his face away when the woman looked at him. Hopeless resignation dulled the woman's eyes. Her under lip trembled.

Happiness in a Madhouse

In the western part of this State there was a woman and she was a good woman. She married when she was young and she had many children; and she nursed and cooked and stinted and kept her nose to the grindstone for thirty years or more. She had, to begin with, sentimental eyes and an imaginative temperament; but her sole recreation during the best years of her life was riding four miles to church every Sunday morning, and her greatest social amusement consisted in feeding the preacher who always wore a goose-quill tooth pick. Her husband died; her children grew up and married; and she, uncertain in her head, was taken to a hospital for those who be mentally unwell. And she found Paradise on earth. She foregathered with a lot of other old ladies who wore their Sunday clothes all the time; sat in sunshiny corners and knitted; talked baby lore and the making of pies; did all things in amity and labored not at all. At length she, too, was cured and sent away--back to the half-deserted home and the ever-present grind. But the memory of the other old ladies with their delightful illusions and their embroidery, and the rocking chair close to the geranium pots, lingered with her and she wept inconsolably. And she, nine times a mother and a woman of consequence in the work-a-day world, made her people take her back to the madhouse. When the heavy doors had closed behind her, she went down the long corridor with a girlish flush on her cheek and a bright light in her eyes. For in the little group that plied needles at the end of the narrow carpeted lane she had found the only rest and peace she had ever known.

The Oldest Woman

The oldest woman in town died the other day. She died happily. She had lived happily--had been "the mother of a church," and had left undone nothing in her small sphere of living. But there is no record of her having been proud of being the oldest woman. The only "oldest" persons who are proud of their lot are those who live in far-away places and hold corn cob pipes between aged gums. For there's pathos here--gaunt, grim solitude. To stand bowed, enfeebled among a strange generation--'tis pitiful, no matter if one's own flesh and blood are close by to lend support. The oldest person! . . . The sun is almost down and there is chilliness in the atmosphere. The eyes rest on a sea of graves. Buried there are all those who could understand. Did you ever know the oldest person? Then you knew one who found happiness only in memory. If the present brings peace and rest, the present can do no more.

The Girlishness of an Old Woman

"Women, you know," said the observant man, "never grow old at heart, though the world forces them to think they are old. They become dispirited through suffering, or embittered through disappointment, or very, very tired through general causes, and they wear the mantle of age gracefully or unprettily, but the spirit of youthfulness remains in the normal woman until she dies. There came to the square the other day an oldish lady, and, as some one spoke to her, her face glowed for a fleeting moment with a girlish flush. The place seemed illumined. The light on her face adorned, yet seemed to defy, the white hair and the marks of care and time, and it was as triumphantly young as the quick leap of a schoolgirl's heart. In the transient expression were kindness, understanding, sympathy. . . . The aged woman tottered to her car; and I began wondering about mankind's universal stupidity and carelessness. Old ladies are too often shelved. People are good to them and entertain them in the best company room and wait on 'em respectfully; but there's not enough love and appreciation for the old lady. Why, an old woman is the epitome of tenderness. She can soothe the hard, dry grief of manhood and prattle gleefully with a child. She is filled with a wealth of feeling and has exhausted no emotion. The touch of her fragile hand is a blessing and caress. If right were right, men could but make love to old ladies."

The Last Touch

Dying must be pretty hard when one can't reach out his hand and touch a woman. Each life is apt to be a solitary, misunderstood thing; and all, or the best of, understanding and comfort can only come just through a woman. A man, in a man's fine strength, may live as a man pleases, but when the great darkness of the Unknown is suffocating his heart . . . there should be a woman who has the right--and a love of her right--to come close and closer and speak in a low voice and gently. Possibly this may seem a plea for the good use of matrimony. It is immediately mindful of how easy it would be to die if a man's mother were with him. For apart from a mother's love, the sureness of love is accidental, or incidental, or of uncertain tenure.

Fallen Women

Fallen women! These are the human beings that the Florence Crittenton Mission wishes to save by establishing a rescue home in this city. The charity undertakes a task that is desperately hard, for since man was born he has placed furthest from redemption women who have sinned. This is one of the just-so things, and we can't reason about it very clearly. Men do not become "fallen," and their degradation is never so complete that they cannot be pulled back into the esteem of their fellow men. All ages have wrestled over the problem, and have inveighed against the unfairness that has been shown women, but the matter remains as it was in the days of the Old Testament. A man may defile himself and yet live to make his fellows remember only his virtues, but a woman who has cheapened herself is blessed beyond hope if she can escape, even after death, the taint of an unmentionable name. This is the bitter, merciless judgment of the world, and it will be the judgment of the world till the world is dead.

All of you have seen the distinction that is made between the man and the woman, and though you may protest, you still continue to assist all people in making the distinction. Two persons--a brother and a sister--left a little home in the country not a great distance from here. The woman was caught in the vortex and passed from hand to hand, but the man did worse than she, though, by his own count and in the opinion of those who knew him best, this was not held to be so. He may return--as he does return--to that simple home, and in his welcome there is never a doubt, question, or reproach. He looks into his mother's eyes and he faces the preacher at church, but there is no trouble in his heart and no sign of guilt on his countenance. But the sister will never go back into that house, and, being typical of her kind, she will never ask to be taken back. In God's eyes she has sinned less than her brother, but her father and her mother will never forgive her, and, worse than all, she will never forgive herself. She belongs to that class the rescue work is trying to touch--a class that may be characterized in pity, not criticism, as forsaken, hunted, haunted, restless, wretched, hopeless.

A woman is a finer and a more precious thing than a man. She feels this without reasoning about it, and the curse of utter blackness comes when she loses her self-respect. She goes down and down, while everybody and everything fight against her, and she never fights for self-recovery. And men nag her with a superb scorn. For all men are Pharisees with women. We hold them to strict account for every misdeed and forgive them nothing--bring them to infamy and, laughing, leave them there. We do this without apology and we will never apologize, for in this matter it is our natural bent to be as remorseless as the grave and to declare that a woman who sins is lost through eternity.

The Girl in a White Dress

On a dreary, rainy night like this the reporter who saw the letter wonders what became of the brown-haired girl in a white dress who ran away from home a year ago, came to this city, and then disappeared. You see, her mother said she was a slender little girl with blue eyes and was very ignorant of the world and its temptations. And a girl like that ought to be found and taken back to her home. But she was not found, and they've no idea where she is. She had wavy, soft brown hair . . . and a clean, white dress. And she must have had innocence in her eyes. The reporter can't forget the picture and he is wondering if the girl can forget it. And if she remembers it, does memory--hurt? . . . A clean, white dress; and it is raining outside, and rain and other things defile--white. Ah, the pathos! A maiden walked forth into a land filled with strangers, and to a maiden a stranger's touch may be rude.

And did the world help to keep the white dress clean? The vainless wonder! Yet 'tis raining bitter hard and there is a great wet gloom. . . . Where is the mother's girl in the dark--this maiden that went out clean and white?

The Rescue Home

So the rescue home has assumed a task that will require all of fortitude and delicacy, and it deserves the large encouragement that should support a heroic cause. Among the unfortunates that the mission will endeavor to reform there are those who will die with the paint on their faces, and alone, as dogs die. But there are others who have not lost good or womanliness, and they are sick at heart with an existence that now offers no release from bondage. They have found that in the long run their way is a disordered way that will permit naught of pleasure, naught of consolation, naught of heartsease; and they would be clean because the wish for cleanness dies hard in a woman. But they are suspicious by training and sensitive beyond their rights, and they must be dealt with carefully. If you would reform a man you pat him on the back and make him sit at your table; but you would visit a fallen woman secretly, and you would consider yourself good if you kept reproach and lashing pity from showing in your eyes. Adopt a new plan here if you wish to do the right, and give to the unfortunates a kindness that does not patronize and a sympathy that is not feigned. They will need, not tracts, but gentleness, and not the preached painting of their scarlet sins, but a tender, insistent holding by the hand and a soft word of understanding. If you are going to do this hazardous thing, then, in God's name, go the limit in love.

How would it do to make the proposed rescue home a place for the prevention, rather than a cure, for the saddest evil in the world? The home proposes to pluck girls from an abyss. Why not make it lift a hand to keep them out of it? That little girl who came here from Reidsville last week, and went hellward in Springs' Alley, was hungry. She hadn't a cent of money. She was in a strange place; she was young, healthy, lonely and--hungry. She is now in Springs' Alley, but suppose she had known that there was some place she could go to and be cared for till she got work to do? Last year a "blue-eyed girl, wearing a clean, white dress," left her home in Cleveland County and came here--alone. She knew not sin. But she was penniless, and in the darkened city there was welcome to her only from foulmouthed hags who trade in human souls. And so the child stumbled on into the night, and her blue eyes became dulled and her white dress was besmirched. Suppose--but why suppose? You know the condition that exists. Continually there come to this town young girls who seek work. They are helpless, ignorant, unprotected. What salvation might come if they knew that when temptation is hardest they can flee to a house of refuge that is gentle and shames not? It is all right to drag the unfortunates from their painted misery, but is it not better to fight for the clear-eyed children who do not want to fall, yet must fall?

The Agony of a Young Girl

"Emma Reese, the girl who swallowed crushed glass, is having convulsions, and, they say, she is about to die," said Sergeant Farrington to an Observer reporter last night at ten o'clock. "I am going to get a doctor and go out to see her. Do you wish to go?" And the reporter, who did not wish to go, went.

Dr. F. O. Hawley, the city physician, accompanied the sergeant and the reporter. Farrington had 'phoned another physician, but the latter said:

"It's no use. There is nothing to do but to give her morphine." But Farrington, as big-hearted a man as lived, was not easy in his mind until he had brought the physician to the side of the suffering girl.

The carriage stopped in front of a small house on Middle Street. Several men stood on the porch and peered into an open door and an open window. Close to the window there was a bed, on which lay a young girl whose white, drawn face was framed in dark, dishevelled hair.

"Will she die?" the reporter had asked.

"If she lives it will be a miracle," replied Dr. Hawley.

And such death--such dying! The beggars, the lowliest who live in all the earth, are given the right to at least die with a certain dignity; but this child is passing within sound of the ribald jest, under the curious scrutiny of bold eyes--passing under the touch of the painted women.

The entrance of the physician, the sergeant of police, and the reporter crowded the small room. Four or five men walked to and fro at will. They did never remove their hats. Why should they? The room was man's common property, and here was only an outcast who was stricken. The women came in kindness, in ministration. They are such as one knows them to be--no better than they should be; guised as women, yet not fashioned to move by death beds.

Privacy! The room was open to the world. The light from the big lamp on the bureau gleamed out into the night and made a beacon, beckoning all men who wandered stealthily by night to come quickly and see the child die. There was no hand to restrain. Here was a rare sight, a man's plaything--a creature that had been rudely broken at life's wheel. So! The spectacle is inviting. 'Tis not every day that a young girl is permitted to die under the full, strong glare of a morbid public.

Chief of Police Irwin came to the scene and cried against the disgrace of the thing. Thrice before he had protested, but to no avail. When he left the house the leering tribe crept back and crouched and waited like so many ghouls.

The girl was indifferent. The spasm of agony had passed under the morphine and she looked out listlessly from tired eyes. A dozen people jabbered at once and she did not listen.

Grossness--if there had been grossness--had gone from a face that was purified by pain. "I am not eighteen, but sixteen, years old," she said, and she seemed hardly so old. As her lithe young body was outstretched to find anxious ease, she seemed so pitifully young. In the entreaty in the dark eyes, in the wearied expression of the face, and in the clean, fresh, white that encompassed her, one found a spirituelle quality, and then lifted his eyes to see the sensualism that suffocated the room.

For a little while the girl was unnoticed except by the reporter. Did she wish to talk? Yes; that might ease her. Then--

"Why?"

"Because I had not a friend in the world," was the reply.

"You see," she continued, "I was not suited for the life I was leading. I came here from Asheville, three months ago, to work in a cotton mill. I did not work in the mill long. After that--after I came here I was always unhappy."

She paused, and a perfumed young girl with curled hair who came to lie on the side of the bed leaned over and said that Emma must not talk if it hurt. But Emma Reese said she wanted to talk.

"Emma Williams, the woman that I live with here, went to Spartanburg," she said, "and I was all alone. I had no money; not a living person to whom I could go about anything. Emma had gotten into trouble, and because of that the police said I must leave town. There was nowhere for me to go. There was nothing for me to do but to die. Relatives? Yes, I have a mother living somewhere--in Dillsboro, I think, but I have not heard from her in a long time.

"The broken glass? Why, I took that because I had nothing else to kill myself with. I tried to borrow some morphine or laudanum, but everybody seemed to know what I wanted with it and they wouldn't let me have it. So I came home and broke a bottle into little pieces and swallowed the cracked glass in a spoon. Oh, but I wanted to die and die quick. I didn't know that the glass would be like it is; I thought I would die before night. And here--

"I don't want to die now. I say, I want to live--so. But I suppose I can't. If I could only take back that--glass. But, I say, what was there for me to do. I was so miserable. And there was no place for me to go. And I didn't have a single friend in the world."

There was nothing for the doctor to do? "I was so miserable." And there was more morphine. 'Tis a restless game of wait. Glass is not quick, but sure and insidious in its methods. For several hours after Emma Reese swallowed the contents of the spoon she felt but little inconvenience, but then pain came in quick, sharp tugs and gnawed fiercely.

"Her condition to-day is worse than it was yesterday," said Dr. Hawley. "I see not the least sign of hope for her."

To-day an effort will be made to take the girl to one of the local hospitals. In mercy she should be taken there. If she lives by any unhoped-for chance, let her recover in a healthy atmosphere; if she dies, in pity's name, don't let her last glance rest on the signs and the habiliments of the painted women.

For no matter what she was, she is now but a child--a poor young girl who is wretched and repentant.

"That is a sad case," said the chief of police, as he was returning from the house. "Three weeks ago that girl told Officer Shields that she wanted to reform, and asked for help. The matter was taken up by Recorder Shannonhouse, and I sent word that I would give the girl a railroad ticket to get out of town. We would have helped her all we could; but in a few days Emma Williams got into trouble, and she and Emma Reese, who was a witness in the case, were warned to leave town. She took the glass on the day she had to leave.

"The law does not protect fallen women, chief?"

"No," replied the chief of police, who, as the reporter knew, is always ready to aid the unfortunates in any possible manner.

"We learn some terrible things," added Chief Irwin. "Two nights ago a white girl from Reidsville, who was so young that she wore short dresses, came to a house in Springs' Alley. The old woman in charge refused her admission, and 'phoned to me. I have tried to find that child, but I can't. She is lost somewhere in Springs' Alley."

Lost in Springs' Alley.

Lost in hell!

CHAPTER VI
CHILDREN

A Baby's First Ride

Swathed in clothes enough to suffocate him, and handled as carefully as if he had been the only jellyfish in the world, a new baby was carried down the steps the other day and given his first view of the world. A spectator, who realized that he was in the presence of an awe-inspiring proposition, took careful note of the surroundings. The only things in sight of the baby after he came into the open were a small negro boy leading a poor cow, a homely man with a red nose, a young woman with an ill-fitting skirt, the iceman, a country dog, and a lot of trees covered with dead, yellow leaves. And the baby cried. Of course he cried. He and the tired woman with the love-lighted eyes had been staying in there together having such a dreamy, comfy time talking and crooning to each other; and he had built a grand vision of the outside, sunshiny place where the birds sang and flowers wafted faint perfumery. And here were the nose, the dog, and the iceman. Certainly he was disappointed and wept and wanted to go back and be with the low-voiced, tired woman. He knew that he hadn't been treated fairly, and he rightly argued that when a baby leaves the dark room for the first time he should enjoy a bigger celebration than any débutante. There should be only beautiful people on the premises, and a wealth of flowers, and somebody should sing a Christmas carol. The formal introduction to the new kingdom where he must live and love and suffer, and suffer and love and live and die should be triumphant and gladsome. For, after all, who can gauge the importance of the first world-impression on the tiny soul--just out from Heaven and soon to creep out from the love-lighted eyes?

A Little Runaway

A young woman of four years of age ran away from her home in this city last week. She went out into the world and stayed for a long time--for her--and when she was found at last and brought back to her home she had nothing to regret, and her memories were fraught only with big adventure and innocent pleasure. The police had a record about a child lost, and afterward a child found, and there was some mention in the paper about the gladness of her parents; and that is all there was of this wonderful episode.

Even a very beautiful poem, with all the right words in the right place, could hardly do justice to the perfect experience of this little woman. Before she left home her world had been limited to her nurse, her people, her toys, and a dozen or so folk who took liberties with her hair and kissed her without being asked to do so. So the little maid mutinied within herself and sighed for the larger freedom which, she imagined, began at the far corner of the opposite block. One day--and it was a very fresh and delightful day, with plenty of sunshine --she waited till the watchers drowsed, and then she wandered into the unknown place. Soon the mystic corner was passed, and the maiden was a stranger in a strange land.

There is no reproach or disappointment to mar the travels of the little lady. She was very tiny, but so confident and fearless in her bearing that no one molested her or asked her why or whither she journeyed. Strange men and women, horses, cows, dogs, children--she passed them all, gaining new impressions at every step. She saw no evil, no unhappiness as she hurried out into the mysterious world. No one held out a detaining hand; she had all liberty, and this never meant anything less than peace, contentment, and, maybe, the fulfillment of ideals.

After the little maid had passed through the world and its madding crowd, it is altogether seemly that her journey should have ended by the side of a brook. She was content to stop here where there were restfulness and quiet save for the murmur of the little river. She was only a mile from home. In her own mind the distance might have been a million miles and a lifetime. And she had nothing to regret. She had seen all that there was to be seen and there had been no disillusionment.

The return home--the greatest of all tests--brought no fear, left nothing in completion of joy. Her faith in the world was so simple and genuine that, after she had become a little tired, she was not at all surprised when a man with a kindly face came to her, lifted her in his arms and carried her to her people. They wept in their gladness, but the maiden's eyes were bright and clear. She was so fresh to life that her own mystery-ideas were not clear, and certainly could not be analyzed; but she must have felt that she had exhausted all of living and adventure--and all was good.

Aye, child, you have accomplished the impossible. You went out, saw all that you cared to see, were not tempted to look in dark places--and came back with fearless eyes, unscarred, not embittered, unashamed. Oh, little girl, what a lesson you teach!

New-fangled Notions About Babies

They've stopped rocking the baby now, and before he is two years old he is taught to say isn't instead of ain't. This is part of the kindergarten system which is death to goo-goo talk, and teaches a child to parse with blocks of wood and toy horses before he has seen five summers. The old-fashioned, fat, clumsy baby who went to sleep while he was being tossed from one end of the room to the other in the hereditary cradle, and awoke to stumble around and mumble, unrebuked, a language of his own--that baby is a back number.

They are saying nowadays that rocking a baby is not at all good for him, and if you keep on rocking him his brains will get scrambly and he will become addle-pated. The modern baby, recently imported, is placed in a stationary basket, just as if he were a newly purchased Maltese cat; and no matter how dear he may look when he blinks his eyes to sneeze, or puts his pink toe in his mouth, nobody ever thinks of leaning over him and telling him he is a tootsie-wootsie. He has three-syllable words pounded at him while he is still breathing out of the top of his head and before he has any backbone at all. Of course this will breed pride, a disinclination to put everything that he sees in his mouth, and an early aversion to mud pies. He is up against an entirely new condition. All, or nearly all, the old black mammies are dead; the young nurses have a grammar school education, and his mother is a member of a latter-day cult which treats an infant as if he were a rational human being.

The subject is not laughable. You go out on the streets any day and you'll see a lot of babies that look as if they had lived in Boston before they were born. They are so proper and knowing-looking. And if you forget yourself and indulge in any of the simpering, minus-g talk that soothed you when you first imbibed out of the neck of a bottle, you are apt to get a dignified, reproachful look that will chill you to your marrow. The modern baby is really very fearsome. Nobody ever sings Him a foolish old plantation ditty; nobody ever edifies Him by crying boo-ah, boo! Nobody even lets Him endeavor to pull the tail out of a cat or toddle around with a face that is sweet beyond his ears and years.

The future only can declare the wisdom or unwisdom of the new plan. "Manhood is but the dusty wareroom where are stored life's broken dreams;" and the journey that began with a fast, jerky ride in a cradle, ended on the first summer day that brought unused shoes to young feet, and included unlimited dirt and goo-goo speech, is the only period in life that is allowed to be perfect.

Miss Daskam

Speaking of juvenile things, have you read the children stories of Miss Josephine Dodge Daskam, the most delightful woman writer in America? In a volume entitled "The Madness of Philip," and containing a number of short stories, she exposes the heart of a child, or the hearts of many children. In all literature the book has no likeness. The majority of authors stoop to write about children, treat them in a patronizing, unknowing sort of way. But Miss Daskam shows the inner emotions of a child's soul, and her words ring true. She is anything else but conventional; but her art is a delicate, beautiful realism. And the true picture of a child is always refreshing.

"Motherhood"

It was Miss Daskam, by the way, who wrote that great, fierce poem, "Motherhood," which appeared in Scribner's last year, and which has been reproduced in this paper, but is reprinted here because it is the most beautiful thing of its kind that was ever written.

"The night throbs on, but let me pray, dear Lord!

Brush off his name a moment from my mouth.
To Thee mine eyes would turn, but they go back,

Back to my arm beside me where he lay--
So little, Lord, so little and so warm?

I cannot think that Thou had'st need of him!
He is so little, Lord, he cannot sing.
He cannot praise Thee; all his lips had learned
Was to hold fast my kisses in the night.

Give him to me--he is not happy there!
He had not felt his life; his lovely eyes
Just knew me for his mother and he died.

Hast Thou an angel there to mother him?
I say he loves me best--if he forgets,
If Thou allow it that my child forgets,
And runs not out to meet me when I come--
What are my curses to Thee? Thou hast heard
The curse of Abel's mother, and since then
We have not ceased to threaten at Thy throne.
To threat and pray Thee that Thou hold them still
In memory of us.

See Thou tend him well.
Thou God of all the mothers! If he lack
One of his kisses--ah, my heart, my heart,
Do angels kiss in heaven? Give him back!

Forgive me, Lord, but I am sick with grief,
And tired to tears and cold to comforting.
Thou art wise, I know, and tender, aye, and good.

Thou hast my child and he is safe with Thee.
And I believe--

Ah God, my child shall go
Orphaned and among the angels! All alone.
So little and alone! He knows not Thee,
He only knows his mother--give him back!"

A Child's Sense of Injustice

"I saw a man mistreat his small son to-day," said the observant resident, "and I know that some day the child will look down the years with a man's eyes and count the thing in his estimate of his father." In his secret heart every living man pities one creature above all others. 'Tis himself as a child. His remembrance of his own first youth may please him; his childhood may have been good and happy; yet his heart will surge with pity for the little unseeing, unknowing person who--whatever he was--was helpless.

All of us are apt to have an acute recollection of the important incidents in our childhood, and the things that meant big pleasure, or suffering, or injustice do not seem smaller as the years pass. A child draws conclusions ignorantly or blindly, but years afterward the man looks back and sees the truth. If he is the right sort of man he will still be grateful for the punishment that was deserved and for his own welfare, but when his hair is white he will not forget the unfairness or harshness that may have clouded his life when he was not more than six years of age. It may be against his will, but he must sit in judgment on all people who reached out hands to touch the life of that child. Matters unheeded then, or overlooked, or misunderstood, rise vividly under the inspection of sober, experienced eyes, and the man knows the truth and must--in spite of himself--place it in the scales that measure the estimate of another's life.

Men treat men with diplomacy and not always with sincerity; but the man remembers that his child's eyes saw men and women as they were. He did not understand them then. He understands them now, and he must judge them now for what they were then. For the memory of childhood does not die. 'Tis the one thing left to him who mumbles at the side of the heart--too old to move. What happened in the rush of manhood was not keenly registered on the passing senses, but the child had seen fresh, glowing pictures that are still seen clearly and understandingly through the mist of the threescore years. And the man whose head is bowed with age must yet brood awhile over the unjust anger or the cruelty that brought pain and humiliation to the tender, pitiful child who lived in the long ago.

Children should be treated not as fools, but rationally; firmly, sternly, if you please, but justly, kindly, and, over and above all, fairly. See! Yonder is a man who is handling his boy as if he were some little tame animal, and he wouldn't hesitate to deceive him half a dozen times a day. Yet if that father would pause to think, he would know that some day his son will see him as unerringly as you and I see him now. And the final condemnation of a child lives till life dies.

Sorrows of Childhood

Do children really suffer mentally? Suffer! Why, there is no agony on earth more exquisite than the suffering of a young child. You are grown up now and think you have forgotten, but you haven't. When you come to die, or in tense moments, you will feel that you have a great white scar that marks the supreme, wild sorrow that possessed your helpless child's soul. Can't you understand the swift, clean agony that came to that little girl as she tottered over to save that burning doll with the eyes of China blue--her doll--her child? Suffer--a child suffer? The man immersed in business cares flinches even now when he looks back on the years and remembers the death of the dog, his dog, that died when he was young and tender--flinches at keen recollection of the cold, bleak sky, the stillness in the atmosphere, and the little dark body that romped no longer but lay cold and inert. The bitter, bitter wail that choked the throat then might have filled a universe with its sadness. Children are the playthings of Grief--a thing that the added years teaches one to fight and, God willing, to subdue.

A Shattered Idol

A great deal has been said about the misfortune that befell L. C. Caldwell, Esq., when he had his false beard burned off while playing Santa Claus at a Christmas tree, and so far everybody has commiserated Mr. Caldwell. But the writer ventures to shed a tear with those little children who believed that Mr. Caldwell, in his rôle of Kris Kringle, had come fresh from the North Pole, and that even the last hair of his billustrious beard was safe from mortal harm. What must have been the horror, not to say disappointment, of the youngsters when they saw Santa Claus jerk that flaming beard from his face and grimace in his exceeding pain? That was enough to inject scepticism and distrust into the youth of the entire community. All a-tumbling came the childish air castles. Fairies became frauds; Jack the Giant Killer no better than a tin soldier; the godmother, a washerwoman. Here was unutterable tragedy. Disillusionment usually comes gradually--as steady, irresistible blows at peace; but in that little room where Mr. Caldwell stood as the living embodiment of the Christmas spirit there was a psychological crash, and even the littlest children saw, by the light that flamed above the beard, that the doll with the eyes of gentian blue was but a bit of wax after all; that the proud little wooden prince sprawled too clumsily at slight gesture. . . . saw, in a mental flash, that the night spirits that hover over tiny beds had wide, sorrowful eyes, and, agonized, were about to flee from the ghastly fire that curled devilishly around a whited beard. Oh, Mr. Caldwell, what a lot you will have to answer for; and how blind you are in thinking that your sins and woes can be cured by the mere application of cold cream!

The Motherless

The community was glad to know that the little children in the Rescue Home are doing well. They are such tiny little ones--all less than six years old. They belong to the class that must be fed as sparrows are fed, and it is good to know that they are housed and cared for in a motherly way. Maybe some of you remember a pitiful little tragedy that was enacted here two years ago. It was the story of a woman and her child--a girlish woman who looked out of wearied eyes and said she was not good enough to rear the baby. There was no denial. She had been broken at the wheel, and she said in a wail that she had forfeited her right to the manchild. Well, 'tis such children that the Rescue Home cares for--tender little children who might otherwise be as friendless and homeless as little--dogs. The great aching cry of the motherless. . . . the home answers that cry, and so is largely privileged and blessful.

Making Children Happy

One of the biggest men in this county came into this place one night and said:

"I have thought it all out; and I know there is no happiness in the world save in giving happiness to other people." And he looked into space and thought and thought. The next day a rollicking, careless youngster picked up little Ben, who drives the Thompson orphanage donkey, and carried him into a drug store and gave him all the ice cream he could eat. There was a world full of sunshine; the birds sang merrily together, and a tender little heart saw only beauty and bliss. Lord--the chance is everywhere--just everywhere.

'Tis an old plaint--this curse of longing for the freshness and the keen appetites of childhood. In one of the local drug stores the other day, a man whose pockets jingled money looked at a little raggedy boy who loitered at the door and watched wistfully the revellers at the soda water counter. His eyes glowed in feverish animalism. There was a dry swallow in his throat and his mouth was parched. He wanted so much to eat and drink those heavenly things that he had to fight down a wail of bitterness. The man beckoned to the boy and fed him to the full. The boy ate like a starved thing, yet gratefully and happily as a prince. He looked enviously at the man who turned his back on the banquet table and who would have given half his possessions to have tasted that moment of satisfied youth. Here is a small tale of life and living. The child dreams that he will find satisfaction complete on the day that he can eat what he likes and do what he likes. When that day comes he is satiated, and he spends a good part of the rest of his life trying to stimulate an appetite that left him when he ceased to go barefooted. Finally . . . "Mush is what I like best," said the late Henry Gratton Springs, who was far past the threescore years and had three-quarters of a million dollars. "I have tried it all, but mush--a plain, simple child's dish of mush is best of all."

Master John Stagg

And Master John W. Stagg, Jr., will be missed, too. That child has the face of an angel and a heart for devilment that has endeared him to everybody in the town.

A Bachelor's Sigh

"Sometimes I know what I have missed," said the confirmed bachelor with a sigh. "I suppose there is only one thing in the world that is worth while. Years ago this friend of mine came to me. His face was flushed, his eyes gleamed, and he was trembling slightly. 'Oh, my God,' he said in a sort of whisper. 'It is a boy, and they put him in my arms and'. . . . 'The mother?' I said. 'The mother,' he replied, 'the mother is all right. The--mother!' He was humbled, yet glorified; and I felt that all the emotions I had ever known counted for naught. That--that is worth more than all the rest. This ache of wanting to be bothered by a baby. . . . "

The New Book Club

Have you heard of the new book club that has been organized in this city? It is called Fame, and it has only four members: Frances Osborne, Annie Dewey Chambers, Mary Osborne, and Estelle Hargrave. If you are half as clever as these little women you will readily see how they got the name for their club. Put in a line the first letter in each name. Ah, you see now, don't you?

The members of this club are between the ages of ten and six years. Which is ten and which is six? You mustn't know, you know. 'Twould be against the dignity of the club to tell an indelicate thing like that.

And, oh, the meetings and meetings they have! Not Maeterlinck! Not George Meredith! Not the Eyetalian poets! Oh, no, of course not. But fairy tales--aye, the dreamy stories of the prince and the princess, the sprites in buttercups, the elfs in wonderland, the nymphs in the dells, the mermaids who sang by the side of the coral reef.

Here's a book club! Never a doubt, never a criticism, never a bit of cold analysis. Alas! It is true--too true that the young nobleman was changed to a big black bear--true about that awful giant and the seven-league boots--true that the slipper and the prince returned to Cinderella. Red Riding Hood! How pathetic. . . . And fairy godmothers are always ready to come out of the next room and do--oh, just anything!

Fame! So. They've all the fame that childhood wants--the precious misty fame that is near to the spirit world--the fame that the older world forgets, forgetting the only pleasure that is complete.

Four little heads bending low; four little souls that know no evil; four little hearts beating in perfect faith and perfect happiness. Dear, simple, unknowing--Fame.

CHAPTER VII
ANIMALS

A Law-abiding Horse

Every few months it becomes the duty of the chronicler of the happenings in this city to devote a special chapter to the sage doings of animals in the community. The last chapter dealt with the loneliness and philosophy of Capt. A. G. Brenzier's tailless Isle o' Man cat; and the history is cheerfully resumed with an account of the wisdom of Dr. R. L. Gibbon's horse.

This horse was hitched to a buggy in front of the Private Hospital yesterday morning when he became frightened by the near approach of a bicycle and ran away. He came at a rapid gait till close to the square, and then he remembered the city ordinance which says that no horse, not even a runaway doctor's horse, shall travel across the square at a greater rate of speed than three miles an hour. So the remembering animal slowed up almost to a walk till he had crossed the hard brick pavement. The brief respite in his race caused his riotous blood to cool, and after he had crossed the square he ran no more.

Two Knowing Horses

And the two horses that pull the Central Hotel 'bus also know a thing or two. The other night when they were at the Southern depot, Charley Lindsay, the porter, not noticing that the driver was not in his box, rang the bell for the 'bus to start up-town. The horses understood the signal, and, with no guidance whatever, came trotting up street, pulling the 'bus free from all collision, crossed at the proper place, came in front of the Central, stopped for a moment, and then gently backed the 'bus around to the curbing for the passengers to get out.

"Judge"

Dr. George Graham has a little water spaniel named Judge that is a rank hypocrite. In the daytime he stays at home and is a proper and respectable dog, but at night he is on the town and is the constant companion of the police. He has fooled his owner sadly, and Dr. Graham little guesses that his prize pup is a runabout. The dog understands the art of deception perfectly. Now, he and Pitts are comrades, and at any hour of the night he may be seen traipsing at the heels of that policeman, but when Pitts happened to go to Dr. Graham's house the other morning, Judge met him at the gate and barked at him furiously. He simply wouldn't be pacified, and made as if he would like to eat Pitts. But there was a roguish twinkle in his eye. That night he stole away from home, found Pitts at the police station, followed him till daylight, and then sneaked home through back streets.

A Dissertation on Cats

Of all the sporting gentlemen, the cat is the sportingest. Who so ready for the chase--who so vigilant and patient? Even more so than an Esquimaux a cat is like unto Izaak Walton. Perchance he sleeps a while on the hearth or climbs to the top of a high fence and lifts his voice in melody, but he ever has the same preparedness for the chase that his forebears had in the jungles thousands of years ago. Such a beautiful life he has! His chiefest ambition is to catch rats, which are forever giving him a delightful surprise party, or else they creep out of holes to reward his exceeding vigilance. Above all other living things the cat does more of what he likes to do. Man and the other animals are curbed, but a cat is a free lance from his earliest childhood. He can go and come when he pleases, and it is the mission of his life to find perfect pleasure in selfishness. But it is as a sportsman that he wins most renown. He counts more scalps than anybody; and with him the joy of the kill and the rapture of the feast are nicely blended. While he purrs under the stroke of civilization he throws back to the old days, and panders to every primitive, barbaric impulse of his nature. He never laughs and he never smiles, never gives affection to anything or considers anything except his appetites, yet the world approves of him. He is the unfairest, sneakingest hunter and the cruelest thing alive, but his methods do not provoke even a frown. He reeks in misdeeds, but is selected as the fit companion for the newly born as well as for the agedly virtuous. Such a gentleman a cat is, to be sure. He defies classification in his own kingdom, and is beyond any comparison except as illustrating well-defined human characteristics. There is no moral to any story about a cat. Cats don't figure in Sunday-school story books or ecclesiastical homilies.

A cat is really a sphinx. No one ever knows what he is thinking about or what to make of him except the witches, and they won't tell. Of course, certain moods are understood. In the heart of a family a cat lies, and sometimes purrs under the last touch of a dying hand; and you know somehow that he is either thinking about torturing a rat or imagining how bully it would be to slay a canary bird. In truth, a cat plays tricks with the human mind. It is not easy to picture an ideal home without thinking of a cat which joins his purr with the lazy hum of the tea kettle; yet in the Dark Lands where nightmare is gendered there is a cat. Where the earth is damp and foul smell is; where one can barely see through a slimy forest and gaze upon a blood-red moon--there a cat is, a mangy, crawly cat with shiny eyes. His image is the dearest plaything of a baby and yet stalks wailingly and unctuously to the dead. One tries to analyze, and then must loathe a cat; and then stops and caressingly lays his hands on that inscrutable face. A glorious, free, unfathomable man a cat is. His song belongs to the after-world, and one knows it will be heard there as a thin treble in satanic chorus. Meantime he is privileged to show the only reeking, flaunted evil that is conscienceless. What a fine contempt he must have for mankind--this unsuffering, remorseless cat whose creed makes him lower than nearly all humanity and bad as the devil himself.

Of course a man doesn't make such a scathing criticism of cats unless he has provocation. For a year or more the comment man has been writing pieces about that big black cat up-stairs in the club, about the bell around his neck and how it cut off his pleasure and prevented him from associating with other cats. Well, he has gone and had four kittens--up there in the room where the nice old colored woman keeps the sheets and things. And it's a crying, mewing shame.

A Spinster's Cats

Cats play a large part in the life of the community. Only last week The Observer related the woes of a lady who had twenty-seven pet felines and yet sorrowed for the death of one beloved, which had come to her death through a small boy and a rifle. All these twenty-seven cats are fat and docile and have no higher wish than to loaf around the house and be scratched on the head. So many cats is surely a thing to be proud of. The only criticism that can be made of these felines is that they are too lazy, not ambitious, too--er--effete.

"Benjamin Tillman"

Mister Bob Jordan has spent several thousand dollars in putting gilt and glitter and mirrors and mahogany and things in his billustrious drug store, and not one cent in the adornment of Benjamin Tillman, his one-eyed cat. Yet Ben with a single optic, a plebeian face and a mussed up back is by far the most conspicuous figure in the store, though he is as much out of place in his surroundings as a bar-keep in the present municipal campaign. Ben suffers from "onwee." He remembers the brave pioneer days when he used to sit in Jordan's front door and engage in hand to hand combat with rats that came from the Central Hotel before the $150,000 improvements had been added to that building. Now Ben, too old to change his home, must forever be studying his own homely physiognomy in multitudinous mirrors, must parade his old shaggy coat as the wretchedest garment at a wedding feast. Ben is like your poor country kin trying to be at ease in your best parlor.

The Black Cat at the Club

A black cat that belongs to the Southern Manufacturers' Club, of this city, wears a jingling bell. He didn't ask for the bell, but they fastened it around his neck anyway. At first the bell frightened him nearly to death, and he had loud convulsions all times of the day and night. But he got used to the noise and now he rather likes it. He comes down here sometimes and sleeps over in the corner of the room for awhile. The first thing he does when he wakes up is to shake his bell, and then he purrs his pleasure at the sound. Truly, it may be said, he has music wherever he goes.

But the bell has brought a great change in his life. He has a remarkably fine nose for a mouse, and before he wore the bell he was a diligent and accomplished sportsman. Now he travels with so much orchestral accompaniment that he can't get within fifty feet of a rat. The sporting instinct is in him strong, but he is running his legs off in a vain chase.

And that's not the worst of his condition. He is a good-looking cat, with a fine, rolling eye, and before he was attuned to music he was a welcome and esteemed member of the best cat society in town. Now no other cat will have anything to do with him. Why, he hasn't had a confidential, heart-to-heart talk with another cat in three months, and he is beginning to suffer terribly from loneliness. You see, he doesn't know what the estrangement is all about, and the other felines are so afraid of that bell that they won't get close enough to tell him the trouble. The other night he climbed upon the fence in the back yard and delivered a rousing oration. He said he was at a loss to understand why his former comrades were showing him the marble heart. He had done nothing wrong that he knew of; he remained the same old sociable, friendly Tom that they used to know so well; and why in the world did they refuse to give him the glad hand? With that he bounced off the platform and went over to attend a catly tea across the way. But so soon as they heard the bell the other cats fled, and again he was left alone. He came back in here and sat down and was buried in thought for a long time; but he seems to have no adequate reasoning power. He hasn't even seen a rat in many weeks, and he realizes that his friends have placed him in Coventry; but he is still delighted with the bell, and doesn't connect it with his present isolated position. That cat is like a lot of people. Only they wear the bells quite knowingly.

The Rooster's Progress

Fagan, the Jew, filled with terror and knowing that he was to be hanged in a few minutes, became profoundly interested in the movements of a fly. And in moods of lesser consequence trifles have interested other men. At five o'clock yesterday afternoon a large red rooster came from somewhere to the square. There were not a great many people on the streets and very little movement of any kind. From Woodall & Sheppard's drug store to Fourth Street that rooster at once became the feature of interest. He did nothing to speak of--just strolled along and stopped to peck at the ground, and seemed perfectly at ease. At Burwell & Dunn's drug store men came out on the street and gazed upon the chicken; a small group of people gathered in front of Fitzsimons's drug store, the Western Union Telegraph Company, The Observer building, the club, and the Buford and Central Hotels, and stood motionless. All eyes were upon the rooster. Men walked out on the veranda of the Manufacturers' Club and looked down upon the stroller. There was absolutely nothing about him to attract attention. Every now and then he lifted his head and kind of chuckled to himself, or peered at folks, but his equilibrium was never disturbed. There was a profound stillness. More men came to the club doors. Men hollered to men 'cross the street, but nobody seemed to know anything about the rooster. At all points the crowds grew larger. As far down as the court-house men stood still and looked up the street. A wagon trotting along a distant block made a faint but clear rumble. People came to up-stairs windows and looked silently at the rooster. Now several hundred people were to be numbered among the spectators. Judge F. I. Osborne stopped at the square and looked down the street upon the departing fowl. The rooster stopped in front of the Buford Hotel and looked Col. Henry Clay Eccles full in the face. Not a word was said; not a greeting was exchanged. There was a deathly stillness. The tension was now strong. Little children were becoming attracted to the scene. Old men and old women stopped and looked. Leisurely the rooster paused when he came to Fourth Street. Slowly and deliberately he turned 'round and glared upon all the countless eyes. Then carelessly, without hesitation, and just as if his mind had been made up from the first, he walked thoughtfully down Fourth Street. And once more the town yawned and lapsed into utter boredom. This was the livest news item of the day.

"Jack"

Jack, the celebrated bull dog belonging to Mr. Osmond L. Barringer, was shot and killed at two o'clock yesterday morning by Mr. George Fitzsimons. Mr. Fitzsimons says he killed the dog to save the life of Shep, his Scotch collie, who has the complexion of Bob, Son of Battle, but whose chief aim in life is to play with the little Fitzsimons children.

Jack met his death merely because he followed the instincts of a bull dog. With people he was gentle and affectionate; but he believed it was his mission in life to slay other dogs and cats, and he fought on sight--fought without any preliminary growling or quarreling. He was as lithe as a panther, and when he met another dog his body went out like a catapult, and he never rested until his teeth were on the enemy's throat and his own eyes were closed for the kill. Jack knew no half-way measures. He wanted to murder.

Shep lives close to Jack's home--the Barringer home--on North Tryon Street, and he seemed to tantalize Jack. Shep is a beautiful dog, with a fine, benevolent eye, and night after night he used to tempt Jack by lying out under the electric light, plain to see, yet safe in a public place.

There is reason to believe that Jack determined long ago to slay Shep. Mr. Fitzsimons dreaded an encounter and he told Mr. Barringer that if the bull dog came to his place and made an attack he would shoot him. Mr. Barringer offered no objection to this proposition, though he and Mr. Fitzsimons agreed that if the collie should go to the Barringer premises and be killed there, there would be no cause for hard feeling. Both men knew--as everybody else knew--that if the two dogs had an uninterrupted meeting the death of Shep would result.

Between the two dogs there was peace, however, until Mr. Barringer left town and went to Baltimore. There was nobody on the premises to restrain Jack's movements, and he celebrated his first night of freedom by attacking Shep in front of the Fitzsimons home. The struggles of the collie aroused Mr. Fitzsimons, who ran to the scene. Jack had not yet warmed up to the fight, and he loosed his hold and fled when Mr. Fitzsimons appeared.

The attack on the collie yesterday morning was as well planned as if it had been the conception of the human brain. The Barringer home was practically deserted, and Jack and a younger bull dog belonging to Mr. Barringer had the free run of the grounds. Standing in the shadow of their yard they could easily keep account of the movements of the collie in the yard across the way.

Up to midnight Shep was seen in front of the Fitzsimons house. Some time after midnight he went around the house and into the back yard. The two bull dogs crept across the deserted street, through the Fitzsimons yard, past the house, and went down on their game.

Apparently Shep didn't have one chance in a thousand of escaping death. After the first rough-and-tumble the bull dogs fastened hard with their teeth--the younger dog on the loins, Jack at the throat. The muffled screams of their pet collie aroused the Fitzsimons children, who raised a wail in harmony. Without pausing to dress, Dr. Joseph Graham and Mr. Fitzsimons rushed out into the yard to the rescue. The younger bull dog saw the men and fled. But the game was now too sweet for Jack to abandon. His hind feet were tugging at the ground strenuously and he was shaking the big collie like a reed in the wind. Shep was still nimble on his feet, and in his sharp struggles to escape he and the bull dog whirled in circles.

The fact that the dogs moved almost as one body prevented the men from shooting for a minute or so. They feared they might strike the collie. Dr. Graham opened the attack and missed. The first two or three shots went wild, and then Mr. Fitzsimons picked his chance and shot the bull dog through the lungs. Instantly a great red splash appeared on the clean white side of the dog, but he only tightened his hold on his victim. Mr. Fitzsimons stepped nearer still and fired, striking Jack just behind the left foreleg. 'Twas a mortal wound. Yet the bull dog only lunged harder for the collie, and his teeth did not relax until he was overcome by weakness. Slowly, gradually, almost with a sigh, he turned the collie loose--stepped back and looked at Mr. Fitzsimons.

"At that moment," said Mr. Fitzsimons, "he compelled my utmost admiration. I started to shoot again, but I couldn't shoot, somehow. He did not cower or seem at all afraid. He looked me in the face for a moment, and then he walked away--straight out in front of the Lutheran church, where he fell on the sidewalk. Then, to relieve his suffering, I walked to him and shot him through the head. He was the gamest bull dog I ever saw, and a bull dog, you know, is the gamest thing in the world."

The news of Jack's death will come as a great blow to Mr. Barringer, who is with the Elks in Baltimore. His love for the dog was passing strong. He had owned the little fellow since he was a tiny pup, and there was a strange sort of comradeship between the two--the man and the dog. More than almost any other dog that the town knew, Jack was like folks. He was a gentleman all the way through, and his politeness to people made him notable. He bothered nothing in the world but dogs--and cats.

In the canine annals of crime Jack has no peer. Even Mr. Barringer has ceased to try to count the number of fights Jack had, but Mr. Barringer knows that Jack has killed in twenty-nine fights and has never been vanquished in any combat.

The presence of Jack alone would have made the Barringer premises famous in a way. If a dog, no matter what kind of a dog, went in there he died nine times out of ten, and if he escaped death 'twas merely because some person happened to be close by to pry open the teeth of the bull dog. No dog, however large, stood any chance with Jack. With the biggest dog he had a method of wriggling in under his adversary's body and making that fatal coup at the throat. Many residents of North Tryon Street still remember the time that Jack went out and introduced himself to the big St. Bernard dog that weighed about one hundred and sixty pounds, was fashioned like a young calf, and belonged to Mr. John Oates. Jack weighed twenty-five pounds, or something like that, and he was trying to kill the St. Bernard by sections, when the big dog opened his mouth and cried so loudly that he could have been heard a mile. He didn't try to fight. He struck his colors at once, and begged for somebody to come and take him away from the Terrible Thing. And it required the efforts of an entire family to save the Bernard's life.

Away from home, Jack fought only on suggestion or because he was ordered to fight. Once he fought in a public place, in Jordan's drug store, and when the other dog had come to breathe like a very sick kitten they poured ammonia on Jack's face, destroying the sight of one of his eyes. Afterward, when a veterinary surgeon took Jack in the rear of The Observer building and cut out the injured eye, the dog lay perfectly still and never whimpered, though he must have suffered intense pain.

Jack was better known than any dog in Mecklenburg county, or, maybe, any dog in North Carolina. He slew ruthlessly, and his death, as it came, seemed inevitable. If he were a man it might be said that he perished by the sword.

Or, better still, Jack died with his boots on.

CHAPTER VIII
CHRISTMAS

Christmas Coming

Christmas is almost here--Christmas, the saddest, sweetest time of the year. It is a period for entertainment and family reunion, and a time when one remembers how old one is, how worthless, and how little he has really accomplished. Heaven here belongs to the tender world that doesn't know the truth about Santa Claus, and beyond that world happiness is feverish and fitful. To the young, Christmas is a million miles away, but as one grows older time's circle moves more rapidly, and finally Christmas follows Christmas too hurriedly. The old people say that only the world is old; that man is ever young; and the mere space of Yesterday is between the young heart that yearned for the filled stocking and the old, feeble heart that may never throb another Christmas day.

Santa-Claus

Christmas again--and Santa Claus. You give and receive, and congratulate, yet for all your felicitation there are moments when the season is sad to you, even while it is sweetest. It is a time when you review not only a year and long for lost opportunities for improvement, but your vision goes further and you watch the workings of a child's mind as it turned from utter faith to disillusionment. First some one told you who Santa Claus was. You were glad to know then, and proud. But you're not glad now when you come to think of it. Unfaith started then. In a mental flash you trace the journey of that child, and you find that there was too much telling, too many people who were ready to break down ideals; and you find that you, too, have helped to destroy the faith of other people. Along the perilous path you have seen the child come to the vital present; not unscarred and with knowledge that is merciless. You and only you know what the child did along the way--only you and God know the blunders, the sins, the selfishness. You see all this because you cannot help seeing it; because at this beautiful season you realize that perfect happiness is given only to little children; and that after childhood must come the fight, the temptation, the fall, the great sorrow. . . . After the thought charity must come. The best spirit of Christmas is Charity-- Charity rising out of remembrance of the long, bitter road that the little child trod.

A Christmas Day in Charlotte

"A merry Christmas and a happy New Year!"

These be immortal words. They suggest happy firesides and blazing logs; the joy of little children; the repeated handshake; the ready offering of charity; the deepening of love; and a sweeter showing of spiritual life.

As the words are written, the voice of the cow bell and the tin horn and the explosion of the torpedo are heard out on the streets. 'Tis the night before Christmas. One can shut his eyes and see the long rows of houses covered with snow; can almost feel the quietude. There is the gathering of families-- the oft-told reminiscences. Some one reads a Christmas story. The youngest child goes to sleep on the lounge. Such things form part of the universal idea of what Christmas eve should be.

But the noise of the cow bell grows louder and louder outside.

A perfect bedlam! It was so all day. Not hundreds but thousands of people thronged the shops; and the streets were crowded with shoppers who lopped over and sometimes blocked traffic in the widest thoroughfares.

The increased shopping was only an emphasized feature of the week. There was more shopping--much more shopping. Before this the paper has called attention to the vast amount of Christmas money that was being spent here. But yesterday, records were broken. Seemingly, all merchants were selling out everything they had. In the stores there seemed to be a veritable stampede, and there might have been a stampede had it not been for the wonderful amount of good nature that was shown everywhere.

Everything was bought and sold in large quantities. One furniture establishment had three hundred orders for delivery in the forenoon.

Hardware stores came under the shower of holiday gold. And the Christmas stores proper--the places where the conventional holiday gifts are to be had--were strained to the utmost capacity just in selling the articles that the merry crowd wished to purchase in a hurry.

The year has been unprecedented in its financial success. Everybody seemed to have plenty of money. Certainly everybody made a pretty pretense of spending plenty of money. Wealth was scattered recklessly. The spectator, keeping tab on some part of the multitude, swore that the shoppers gave far less than usual thought to purchases. Money came readily out of pocket, and flowed quickly in the general effort to satisfy the municipal Santa Claus. The evidence of prosperity was the keynote of the day. Charlotte had relaxed and was showing itself and the world that it was rejoicing in the commercial blessing.

This suggests the inner condition--the general bias. Everybody seemed glad to see everybody else. Laughter was heard every five feet. Old friends were returning and receiving warm welcomes. The faces of little children were radiant with happiness. The spirit of Christmas was perfect in a heartfelt way.

The purely physical aspect of Christmas eve was bewildering. The noise beggared description. The little boy touches off a firecracker, and fires a cannon, or yells at the top of his voice. That is the ideal concomitant of Christmas. But it is marvellous when all the sound that can be made by ten thousand or more people moving in a small area is drowned by the sound of a cow bell. But that is what happened. It is not known how the cow bell mania started here; but there is a tradition to the effect that once, when the police shut off all noise, Armistead Burwell, Jr., who was quite a lad, bought a cow bell and gave vent to his surcharged feelings by trailing it half a block. That was sufficient to create the disease--started the epidemic, just as Buffalo Bill's show blanketed the town with measles.

The only extra business stand that was erected during the holiday season was for the purpose of retailing cow bells. Their use is odd. They are not held aloft and waved as a token of jubilation, but are dragged in a bumpety-bump sort of manner along the pavement carelessly or apathetically, and yet the effect is such that the composite sound that goes to the heavens from Charlotte is that of a cow bell trying to blend harmonies with a tin horn.

Youth and age meet here on the dead level with a cow bell. Col. R. O. Colt cracked his heels together at the square, whooped in the fulness of his joy, and jangled his cow bell. Little Lacy Seawell did likewise. A colored girl with a green hat and a pink waist sniffed the air because her cow bell was as good as anybody's. The society women and the factory girl found democracy in the bell.

The noise was devilish and incessant.

Jubilation was unchecked, and the police merely confined themselves to a diligent effort to keep the street as passable as possible. From eight till eleven o'clock last night nearly every foot of space at the square was covered by surging humanity that held noise-making as a common object. Confetti was dashed into the face of anybody. There must have been people at home; but the local world seemed to be on the streets. Never was such a Christmas in Charlotte.

The day was without sensational incident. In all the melée no one was seriously hurt. Beyond the arresting of those who drank too deeply, the police had very little to do. Out of a hurrying crowd on East Trade Street came a burly negro who fought hard against several officers. The crowd held its breath momentarily. Then an officer swung his club hard into action, and there was the splutter of blood--the end of the struggle. The offender joined others of his kind at the station, where stentorian voice or heavy, soggy snores tell the tale of ineffectual pleasure.

But the day, taken altogether, stood for success. The beginning and end of it showed a wonderful degree of prosperity; or to quote Mr. L. W. Sanders, "It was the best Christmas Charlotte ever had."

To-day the note of the cow bell will be resumed as the only pronounced sign of celebration. In keeping with the real spirit of the hour there will be much hospitality here--many family dinners and reunions. And, of course, there will be the usual service in all the churches, with unusually good music everywhere.

Such is the general outline of Christmas in Charlotte. No one feature rises up for special notice except the happiness that is the result of money-making and money-spending. As a token of the times the cow bell has the right of way. If there is peace in you, and you, the cow bell and the tin horn may not speak it, and it may not come, individually, as a part of the flush of money. Here are the mystery and the wonder. But--

"A Merry Christmas and a Happy New Year."

Reflections

One wonders what Christmas means to the other fellow. To children it is Paradise transplanted, but men and women view it differently. To some it is a time for love and charity; to others a time for envy and discontent. To some it brings the jubilation that came finally to old Scrooge; to others it brings boredom.

To a composite element of mankind Christmas is a long space relieved from tediousness by a family dinner that provides two helpings of rice and gravy, not mince pie and sleepiness. Your oldest relative once more tells the story of your most youthful folly, and afterward you go into the parlor and pick away at the nuts and raisins and things that rest in a bowl and decorate the centre table. The youngest child in the house brings you a fresh, smelly story book, to read upside down; everybody resists an inclination to stand up in front of the grate and stretch; and somebody goes over to the piano and plays "The Blue Bells of Scotland" with the right forefinger. A man from a distance has sent the daughter of the house some American Beauty roses, and she busies herself by carrying these from room to room, humming as she walks. Out in the hall you hear children from over the way bragging to your children about the superiority of the gifts that were in their stockings. When you go to bed that night you feel as if you had spent the day at a circus where they didn't have any clowns; and, moreover, your sheets feel chilly and dampish. Sheets always feel like that on Christmas night, somehow or other.

Christmas is like any other gala day or a big reception. To find pleasure you must have it inside yourself. This statement might seem unnecessary if it were not for the fact that in the matter of happiness the vast majority of people are utterly without personal resource. They must have happiness thrown at them, or absorb bits of it here and there; and when they are forced to subsist only on the lights and thoughts that God has given them they very properly perish with ennui. The empty fool in search of amusement touches you at every corner.

You see, there is such a hue and cry over Christmas, and when the day comes it may easily bring unsweetness--that let-down feeling of disappointment. No one is allowed to approach Christmas soberly or dispassionately. A few weeks beforehand life may be in placid waters, but as the time of celebration draws nigh the stream becomes a swift current and then a vortex that whirls to and fro the universal multitude clutching holiday gifts. When the storm ceases, if you are a woman and are satisfied with what you've got you are a miracle; if you are a man and can pay for what you have given you are a blessed exception. This is Christmas with the varnish off-- Christmas described in remembrance of home-knit socks that didn't fit; inevitable indigestion; wet fingers that plastered pink candy; useful donations that weren't useful; and the same old snowbird on the same old white card.

All this is intended as a bare touch of realism--a kindly, though maybe a pessimistic, silhouette. The setting may be tiresome, but it will be gorgeous if you have that happy heart. The man who wants the day to give him something will find it a failure. It is a success when the individual assumes that it is his duty to bring to the day love, charity, sympathy, peace.

And, while absorbing the cardinal virtues, he should charge himself with the obligation of bringing to Christmas one other quality. That is understanding--a thing that sermonizing takes into too little account. Your enemies are very often a tribute to your strength of character, and malice may be fought in the open. Richard Harding Davis has one of his characters to say that it is the well-meaning fools who cause most trouble; and there are other varied characterizations of kinds of folk who constitute the most disagreeable citizenship. But the people who do not understand, wilfully do not understand, do the greatest evil. It is a common privilege to speculate as to the punishment the other man will receive in the hereafter, and it is respectfully maintained here that a particularly warm hell belongs by right to those persons who go around declaring motives where there aren't motives, and make a lifetime business of trying to break hearts by misunderstanding. Every one who takes himself seriously and conscientiously would like to shield his life and his work from this class, which are like half-fed vampires brooding pleasurably over suffering and toil. These be the people who enter your house through the front door and are given the seat of honor at your table, and right knowingly they take the things you say and the things you do and, in distortion, flaunt you and covertly taunt you to your hurt. The greatest tragedy is not death, but a miserable life, and misunderstanding causes more misery than anything else in the world.

To try to understand the other man--this, also, should be a very sacred and tender duty. Apart from religion, fairness is the one thing that makes life bearable; and understanding is fairness.

"God bless us all," said Tiny Tim, and the saying beautifies a universe at this season. Maybe God will not see fit to bless all of us, and therefore puny man's duty to his fellow man is larger and better.

CHAPTER IX
SOUTHERN LIFE AND MANNERS

Tribute to the Old North State

"But one of the finest speeches I ever heard in my life," the Old Man continued, "was delivered by 'Gentleman' George Pendleton--Senator George H. Pendleton, of Ohio. He spoke in Charlotte on a 20th of May about 1878, I think; and it was in the address that he paid this memorable tribute to North Carolina:

"'Without great cities or uncultivated wastes, without an excess of riches or degrading poverty, she has provided a University for the education of her sons, and has always known how to tread that middle ground of dignity and of honor and of self-respect without which no State is permanently built.'"

Illiteracy

The educational conference is about the biggest thing that has come this way in a long time, and it will result in putting a good many dollars into the schools of this county. After hearing the statement of Dr. Wallace Buttrick, of the general educational board of New York City, it would be difficult to raise any objection to the gift. He said, in effect, that the best man is down here and promised more in development than any other, and he begged to be allowed to help, just as a brother. The privilege was granted, and Mecklenburg County began a new chapter in history.

The episode was sad, somehow. It is no little thing to proclaim to the world the illiteracy of this State; to discuss and berate unfortunates who cannot talk back. The realization of wretchedness was too vivid. The portrayal of it reminded one of a father who needs must whip his son in public.

It all seemed necessary--but, oh, the shame of open shame! To be sensitive, proud, reticent, and then to be held up for universal pity! 'Tis the rough cut of a surgeon's knife.

Wasted?

Mr. Walter H. Page said there had been enough brains and character wasted in North Carolina in the last one hundred years to have managed the civilized globe. Wasted! Yes, the people have lived simply and raised big-hearted children. Countrymen have kept open house and independence, and have envied no man. And there be, in little towns in this State, men who wear long coats and slouch hats. They have the accent of an English lord, the manners of a courtier, the straight strain of high Saxon breed. They be gentle, brave men, who might have ruled a world and are content to govern a family. And for twice a hundred years, if one has been sick in a hovel in the North State, women have come and tended and blessed. Wasted? Not quite that. Development will come surely and everybody will be educated; and North Carolinians, "nationalized," will go out to conquer by bigness. Meantime, thank God for the waste.

The Simple Life

'Tis an old question, revived by a letter that wondered why anybody could be content to stay in Charlotte or smaller places when New York, Boston and other larger cities offer so much more broadening influences and so much greater facilities for ambition. The letter came from a man who has lived in New York only a year or so and talks glibly about the various streets, Weber & Fields', and a few well-known cafés. Men who know New York thoroughly and are known in that city do not usually advise other people to go there to live. The metropolitan enthusiast is the new resident, who will never know one-tenth as many people as he knew in his native village. He becomes dazed by the glare and glitter, the big sounds and the mad tumult, and calls all this a part of seeing and learning and living and broadening.

But is the city life more broadening than the life down here? Does it give a man a more comprehensive view of life? This question does not consider the genuine cosmopolitan type--the man of the world who may live in New York or anywhere, and who is broad because he has found how utterly small he is and simple because he has learned that any manner other than simplicity is absurd. But does the man who leaves this section of country, for instance, and goes to New York to live--does he enter a broader or a narrower life? Has he a right to pity those that are left behind?

What does the city give the rank outsider? What profit does New York offer the man from our midst who goes there to live? He is swallowed up, lost from view immediately, for--saving a brilliant few--who ever heard of a man who lived in New York? He is a tiny thing who rubs elbows with strangers. He sees millions of people every day, and is lucky if he gets an opportunity to study and know half a dozen. He has no neighbors. In the quick rush there is scant time for sympathy, and his eyes, seeing no further than camera lens, can take no intimate account of the undercurrent --the pulsing human nature that is about. He is on the outside of everything--a little, worrying atom that must fight fiercely for space. He may make a lot of money and spend it extravagantly, but who cares or who notices? He may do a very fine thing, but the man who lives next door to him will never hear of it. The note of his suffering or his happiness is not heard above the ceaseless din, and his death will be no more than the passing of a dray horse. He may successfully pander to fastidious appetites, but does he learn anything that is worth while or do anything that is endurable? He is hurried in a rut, goaded too fast for reflection, keyed up to a point where he confuses personal values. He is a drop of oil in a mammoth machine, or--to change the figure--he reminds one of a bit of scurrying chaff in a maelstrom. Aye, who ever heard of a man in a city? And you, and you, know that the narrowest man who walks these streets is not the denizen of Paw Creek, but the man who has left Paw Creek and smirks complacently when he returns, after having served prenticeship as galley slave to metropolitan drudgery.

The man who is pitied--how does he fare? He stays down here and lives what the world terms a small life, but is his living as narrowed as the city man thinks? His amusements are limited; he is apt to do the same things day after day, and he is not apt to make a great deal of money, but he learns to know a great many people, and to love and be loved by a few. He gets close to a scattered multitude that finds time to be quiet occasionally, and he sees people, not as they seem to be, but as they are. If he is happy there are those who will rejoice with him. If he suffers, men reach out their hands and touch him understandingly. Be he ever so small a figure, his movements are not unheeded; and his virtues, as well as his sins, are a matter of public knowledge. If he does anything that is good and praiseworthy his community knows it and applauds, and he climbs not very high on the ladder of fame before his State sees him and nods approval. Old men and old women stop him and bless him in memory of his father and mother; he knows a countless number of babies; and his neighbors' dogs come out and recognize him as a beloved friend. The joy of his acquaintances is so near to him, so undisguised, that he is gladdened with its radiance, and his eyes are wet in thought of their sorrows. He has time for reflection, and he learns to know his fellow man--know his strength and his weaknesses; learns to commend the one and condone the other. On week days he speaks to hundreds of people who call him by his first name; on Sundays he worships with a congregation that has known him since he was a babe in arms. When he grows old he is not in the way, and when he dies men bring sympathy to his children and declare a common loss. Maybe he, too, has lived in a rut, but he has lived with his heart-side throbbing; he has been an integral part of the life that was builded around him; and the best of him is proclaimed while he lives and lives after he dies.

Both types are exaggerated, but which of the two really lives the broader life?

And the delocalized Southern woman is a pitiable, abortive creature. Mrs. Pembroke Jones, from this State, and some other women from Baltimore, Richmond, and New Orleans, are occasionally heard of in the metropolis, but nine times out of ten the Southern woman in New York has much less social pleasure than she found at home, and she has no tale of triumph to carry back to the South. She gains, however, if she absorbs the best of life about her without losing her own individuality. But she is lost if she becomes an imitative onlooker. Too often she does this. This type you also know and you don't like it--as a type. It is tailor-made, spick-and-span, and conscious to a wonderful degree. It wears three dresses a day down here and talks New York incessantly--tells you about the life there with the same gusto that one would exhibit in describing the habits of a newly discovered tribe in the South Sea Islands. "We do this in New York," or "We do that in New York"--we, the lessees or proprietors. You know the patronizing language. And then the change in the manner and in the voice--that is simply horrible. The best voice that the Lord ever put into a woman's head is the soft Southern accent--the velvety voice, as Miss Mary Johnston terms it. And this is sacrificed by a delocalized feminine product that hasn't even intelligence enough to know that it has cast away its best possession. "She has been to the Big Place and she has come home to see her folks," and doesn't she usually worry you to death? In all these fine clothes you see unnaturalness. The Southern woman is gone, and in her stead you see a person who wraps her clothes around her to show curves, prates unmusical, borrowed speech, and looks above the people who, being merely natural, could reach a social status that she, an anomaly, can now never hope to attain here, there, or anywhere.

All this is a tribute to the folk who have seen, but not enough; who have travelled, but too little--a tribute to fledgelings who return with a strange, harsh crow.

Oh, these people who come down here and talk about the big people they know somewhere else! Why? Why? You meet a decent sort of chap, and just when you are beginning to like him he clears his throat and says, "That reminds me of something Senator Blank said to me once." And you want to take a club and kill him. When a man goes to a strange place he commits a fatal mistake by pretending to know anybody worth while who lives elsewhere. He may be telling the truth in his boast, but nobody believes him. This particular kind of an ass is getting to be so common around here. He makes one weary, sick. A stranger has no business with either people or mighty friends. He is sized up like any other animal, and if he is considered a thoroughbred it will not be because he named his sire. Mankind has a varied creed, but all men, from the beginning of time, have had a quiet contempt for any man who bragged about birth or discussed his nearness to the Distinguished.

You know the class. They return overly dressed and they don't know what to do with themselves. They work hard to kill time in the village; they yawn a good deal; they bore others and are bored. At one time they went barefooted in the town or walked behind a mule in a furrow, but they can't understand now why every resident doesn't sell out bag and baggage and move to New York. They derive their only pleasure while here from meeting some other person who can talk New York with them, and, for the edification of the rural population, they eagerly exchange inane reminiscences of Weber

& Fields, or of some restaurant where one can get a tip-top supper after the theatre. They have gone from this place and have been jammed into some little niche in the metropolis, and they wander back, conscious of a superiority that impresses no one else. In the big city they spend most of their life in offices, and in leisure moments they move among vast hordes of strange people. They call this living and learning; and they go back to their birthplaces to pity--but, above all, to be pitied.

Northern men have voluntarily come here to live and have lived here contentedly without making unfair comparisons. They have been glad to get the freer life that allows time for reflection and for the cultivation o one's fellow man. And on the other hand, the best men in the city are the big-lunged active fellows from the country--men who absorb ideas with wide-open eyes and without being deceived. But the most patent type of ass that one meets down here is the country boy who has moved into the hurly-burly, and, fascinated and bewildered by the din about his ears, loses the proper reckoning of the bigger social values. In other words, a native New Yorker or a Boston man is not apt to bore anybody, and, moreover, he is apt to be at home everywhere; but half of the Southern boys who have barely tasted New York and return home for the holidays ought to be slain for sheer idiocy and conceit.

"The natives who go abroad, spend three months travelling in Europe, and then return to tell you about the well-dressed women in Paris, the height of the tower in London, the pigeons in Venice, or of the nobility in Rome, are of great educational benefit to the provincial State," remarked the observant man. "One may have read much about the interesting sights on the Continent, but it is very gratifying to run across a friend who has seen the things with his own eyes.

I have noticed in recent times that foreign travel doesn't seem to make as much impression upon North Carolinians as it did in former years. A quarter of a century ago you could count upon the fingers of one hand the natives who had crossed the Atlantic. These were mighty men after they returned, and were the central figures wherever they went. 'Why, he's been to Europe!' would be the awe-stricken whisper; and then everybody would hang on the words of the fortunate traveller. Folks knew London through Dickens, and Egypt by the geographies, and personal testimony of the existence of both places was a passport into any and all grades of society.

And foreign travel affected North Carolinians more in the old days than it does now. Why, there was a Mecklenburg man who spent three weeks in Paris, and when he came home he couldn't call an apple by anything but a French name. Another county man who stayed a year in Germany returned speaking broken English. He would say: 'Big gates! Pass me--oh, donder and blitzen, what shall I say? Oh, I remember; pass me dot--what you call heem?--dot bread?' And that fellow had walked behind a mule in this county and in Cabarrus until he was over twenty years old. He was wonderfully proficient with his German, however, and could spot out line after line, from his Ollendorf, about the red dog and the blue cat.

The Old Southern Lady

There is one type that the writer rejoices to have seen before he dies. 'Tis the old Southern lady. In her one sees the elegance and composure of a princess. Viewed surface-wise, she is as a rare cameo--like fragile porcelain in her fineness. In her yet live sympathy and understanding; and she will not let romance die, nor faith, nor the fair idealization of love. You would like to bend and kiss her hand--you know not why. You may seek her as the best companion of youth; the most tactful comforter; the tenderest philosopher. Her liking is a blessing; her love, a mantle that would shield from all hurt. She exacts little and would give so much; offering the clean, unselfish strength of completed womanhood to bring the peace that looks out of her own eyes. She is the most wondrous, yet the most natural and most graceful, picture in the South. You have seen her--this old lady? She is very human as she sits there and gazes out at the dying sun. And yet there is about her a hush, a quietude that seems over and above the things of earth and nearest to Heaven itself.

The Gentleman of the Old South

Mrs. Patterson ventured to say that North Carolina men have the best manners in the world. Which is really equivalent to saying that the best type of the Southern man has the best manners in the world. That is true. They are better poised, easier and gentler, have nicer voices, and are more apt than any other men to consider the little wants and finenesses of women. But this is true, isn't it, Mrs. Patterson? The modern Southern son hasn't the manners of his father. He lacks something and laughs at the lack of it. He is bolder, and not so composed. The old prints which show the features of men of the Colonial days portray a grave, distinctive something that might be termed the spirit of the Revolution. That passed. On the faces of the ante-bellum men there is an expression just as fine, but not so severe. It is warmer; suggests a bow that might have graced a French salon in the old régime; speaks silently of velvety voices and utter deference. Does the Southern man of the present generation face this picture equally, appreciatively? Or is manner a virtue that comes with time, and is it the rightful privilege of youth to shrug its shoulders at the insistent courtesy that is worn so easily by him whose eyes are dim and whose hair shows the touch of frost? What dignity will there be in a portrait of the present generation? The writer has seen, with curious, democratic eyes, a prince and a good many noblemen. They seemed not to be grandees. They were not fussy or haughty. They had the same simple manner that is worn by the older gentlemen of the South. And, mark you this, the Southerner can uncover his head as the social peer of any living man. At least, his father can. The standard of manners may never change, though it may be lowered. It is being lowered with an ignorant laugh. Watch the maid and the man on the street and then observe how old people speak together. And the laugh must give way to a sigh.

Provincialisms

Outsiders sometimes laugh at the "yes, ma'ams" and the "yes, sirs" of the South, and it is noticed that frequently Southern boys and girls who attend the Northern schools come back to face the aged with a too-simple "yes" or "no." Lord forbid that the terms should pass. They belong to the South--belong to Thomas Nelson Page's women; they are part of the speech of the hovel and the pundit caste. The words are used most prettily by young women to old women, and are the peculiar property of the rich, soft Southern voice. They are the young man's quiet show of deference to the old man; the old man's occasional proffer of dignified politeness to the young man. This speech--this habit of language that was learned in the old, old house with the big white pillars--can only be used properly and gracefully down here. And it must always be used down here.

The Educational Awakening

"There's a revolution in this State," said a man the other day. "It is quiet but unmistakable. North Carolina is leaving the back seat of illiteracy, and the people--and especially the young men--are thinking for themselves. The revolution is along educational lines and will result in independence of thought. Ten years ago it was an easy matter to draw the applause of a large crowd by a rancorous partisan speech. That kind of talk met with no favor in the last few political campaigns, and will be coolly received in the future. The people are fairer and honester in politics. The spread of schools and increased reading have caused individual opinion to be more pronounced and more reliable. In other words, the masses of the people are tired of having leaders, whether in politics or business or other matters, think for them. The time is coming when the yell of prejudice and little interest will act as a boomerang. The revolution is reason. The curse of the State is the cheap politician, and he will be the victim of the revolution."

The Thin Gray Line

The Confederate veterans who returned yesterday from the reunion at New Orleans were as pleased as school boys over their trip. It seemed to revive in them youth that easily resists the heavy hand of time. Yet a quarter of a century hence weekly papers here and there in the South will display headlines over an article which will relate that one--just the scattered single one--veteran still lives and remembers clearly some part of the great struggle between the States. The thin gray line is vanishing rapidly, beautifully; and as the years pass one sees that smaller and smaller places may hold all that is left of a host that once made a continent tremble with its march.

Freedom of Speech

"Speakers and writers who look back upon the present year in North Carolina may wisely conclude that they had better be careful about what they say or write," said the observant resident. "There have been vast liberty of speech and vast liberty of criticism; and more than once the pulpit and the press have turned in full cry upon a man and have tried to hound him off the face of the earth. But a man needn't be afraid unless he ought to be afraid. He can be as bold and radical as he pleases, but if he has common sense and tries to be fair his utterances will not hurt him in the long run. The intemperate fool and the insincere extremist are the fellows who sink under attack. In other words, all this war of words and invectives needn't make anybody feel frightened or pessimistic about the liberty of the press or the liberty of the pulpit. Every man holds it a privilege to cuss the other man when he pleases, and he is apt to do this publicly when he is given opportunity, but the man who has provocation to speak can snap his fingers contemptuously at all the yelping crews of critics. The public is not going to misunderstand; and every unjust attack upon a man helps him finally. 'Be sure you are right and then go ahead' is a maxim that people quote sagely, and every man imagines that he is the only man who can live up to it. But if you try to be right you are safe enough. Any man who dares to raise his head above the commonplace will find people who are ready to slap his face, but if he is unafraid and speaks truth as his own heart and mind teach it to him he can die triumphant over wiser men and the fools who would badger him by disagreement."

CHAPTER X
ANECDOTES

Not a Beehive

Maybe you have heard this joke before, but no matter. A young couple went on their honeymoon and stopped at a hotel. He went downstairs to smoke. He came back in a dreamy, sentimental mood, and, opening a door, looked into dark space.

"Honey," said he.

There was no reply.

"Honey," he cried again.

Silence.

"Honey," he said in a louder voice.

Then--

A bass voice came from the blackness, saying: "This ain't no beehive, you dam' fool. It's a bath room."

Outflanked

Col. Peter Akers, the celebrated auctioneer, who was in Charlotte last week, tells a story that he declares is original and has never been published. He was a Confederate soldier and fought under Stonewall Jackson, and loves most to talk of that leader.

"Jackson," said he, "was the greatest military genius the world has ever seen. With a handful of bare-footed men he flanked large armies and whipped three or four armies in a day. His genius was displayed oftenest in that flank movement.

"When he died, St. Peter sent two angels for him. They searched the field, the hospitals--the whole army, but could not find him. They returned and told this to St. Peter. Said he, 'Why, he has flanked you both and has been here six hours.'"

A Remarkable Pony

Addressing a select audience the other day, Mr. George Stephens said: "A friend of mine once bought a Texas pony that was covered with hair so long that it trailed on the ground. He told his man to cut off the hair and bring the beast around to be inspected. His directions were obeyed and the pony was soon clipped clean. He was the most remarkable looking thing you ever saw. From his head to his tail he was covered with x, y, z, and other letters--marks of branding. 'I perceive,' said my friend, 'that this Texas steed is suffering from an eruption of quadratics.'" Mr. Stephens paused, turned around once, and he was alone.

Anticlimax

There is something pathetic in the story in The Stanley Enterprise about the doctor who murdered two partridges, thinking they were hurting his crop. He found, however, that their craws were full of cinchbugs and cut-worms--and nothing more. After the birds were little corpses the doctor found that they were his good friends--had done nothing but spend their time in destroying the enemies of his crops. Poor little Bob Whites--poor little victims of ruthless man's conceited power! They were slain out of season--in the heyday of love-time. Ah, what a chance were here for a tender poem were it not for the cinch-bugs and cutworms. "He died," a letter once ran, "in peace and with his eyes fixed on the Great Beyond; he died of cholera morbus."

An Interview with Cleveland

Some one said the other day that ex-President Cleveland never forgot anything, and this reminded the writer of an incident which may be mentioned, with an apology for ringing in his own personality and that of two other North Carolinians. He was with his father and Senator Ransom when they called on Mr. Cleveland in Washington during his second administration. In the course of the conversation Mr. Cleveland said:

"Judge Avery, what sort of a man is Mr. Blank?" Mr. Blank was pretty well known as a candidate for a certain appointive office. Before Judge Avery could reply Senator Ransom said:

"Wait a minute. Tell him the truth and the whole truth, the good and the bad--all you know. Let me tell you something. Sometimes I have come into this room here and have asked Mr. Cleveland to give an office to a certain man. I have praised the man up to the skies--credited him with all the virtues and no faults. And then the Old Man (pointing to Mr. Cleveland) would say:

"'But, Ransom, didn't your man steal a sheep on such and such a day, in such and such a place--or something like that?' And the man had stolen the sheep," concluded Senator Ransom. While Senator Ransom was speaking Mr. Cleveland looked at him with an appreciative smile on his face. Then he turned to Judge Avery with a question mark in his eyes, but said nothing. And Judge Avery, of course, proceeded to declare that if the gentleman in question had stolen a sheep, it was a very small sheep indeed, and should not be reckoned with in the judgment of a man who despised mutton on principle.

They Got the Money

"Tom Reed, the Republican leader, is an oddly frank, attractive man," said Mr. D. A. Tompkins. "When he was Speaker of the House I was one of a committee that went to Washington to ask a $250,000 congressional appropriation for the Atlanta Exposition. We had an audience with Reed and briefly stated our wishes. 'Why, certainly. I'll help you to get the money," said the Speaker. 'And you'll get it, too. You dear Southern people so often come up here and make demands on an abstract principle of your rights that it is a relief and a pleasure to listen to those who discuss only their interests and want the government to aid those interests.' And Mr. Reed saw that the money was forthcoming as soon as possible," added Mr. Tompkins.

Repartee

"What do animosity mean?" said a Charlotte servant girl.

The meaning of the word was explained.

"Well, I jess wanted to know. I was er talkin' to er fancy nigger last night and he said:

"'Does de pleasures of de evenin' excite your animosity?' En he had me."

"What did you say?"

"I said: 'Dey sho' do reprehend my sagacity.' Nen I had him."

He Paid for His Pie

Rev. Plato T. Durham, teacher of Bible in Trinity College, studied theology in New York and elsewhere, but it was while in New York that he began thinking of the Waldorf-Astoria. He was vigorous and young, and, as the Iredell County gentleman puts it, he was usually hungry for something to eat. He made up his mind that some day he would stroll down to the Waldorf and order a big, fine, handsome meal, including the French dishes. Finally he made the trip. He turned up his nose at the smartly dressed servants, looked blasé, and summoned a yawn or two to the rescue. A dignified waiter handed to him a ménu card. He gazed upon it listlessly and his mind went blank. Mr. Durham read down the printed sheet. He was hungry. Gilded lights shone about him. The tall waiter leaned over attentively. Mr. Durham cleared his throat delicately, realizing just where the French accent should fall, and then said sternly:

"Waiter, you may bring me a huckleberry pie." The waiter seemed dazed, but departed. Mr. Durham wished to crawl under the table to hide his shame. But the deed was done. Here in a second he, who had gone barefooted in huckleberry patches in his childhood but had never thought of a huckleberry in ten years, had been smitten by the latent childhood in him, and while the voice of a bejewelled blonde in a room across the way was singing classic song there he was a-sitting and a-waiting for a huckleberry pie. Oh, he stood by his guns and ate the pie. He found it was a seventy-five-cent huckleberry pie. He tipped the waiter and strode back to the college, where he ate corned beef with a full heart.

Epitaphs

Major O. M. Sadler stood at the square and expressed his opinion of the weather after the manner of an old Jack Tar who was rounding the cape in a storm. He added that he didn't like epitaphs. "Give me," he said, "a few flowers, but no words. The only epitaph that ever appealed to me very much was this:

"'Here lies the body of John Smith, accidentally shot as a mark of affection by his brother Jim--with one of Colt's revolvers, old kind, brass mounted, and of such is the kingdom of heaven.'"

"The only trouble about that epitaph," said Col. John R. Morris, "is its lack of the pathetic. It contains a beautiful sentiment, but it hasn't the mournful ring that adds so much to the effect of an affectionate epitaph. Let me call your attention to the tenderness in the following statement which I found on a tombstone:

"'Here lies the mortal remains of John Henderson, whose parents were drowned while on their way to America. Had they lived they would have been buried here also.'"

"Or this--

    "'Little Johnnie Leach has flitted from our reach,
    He went away beyond the shining river,
    But we know he's better off, for he had an awful cough,
    And was threatened with congestion of the liver.'"

The Judge's Memory

If you ever happen, by any chance, to find Judge F. I. Osborne in a mood when he is not thinking about something else and wants to talk to you, it will be worth while to listen to what he has to say. He is a man who remembers everything he read twenty-five years ago, and laughingly agrees with Sir William Hamilton's idea that one forgets nothing, though he may not recall everything that he remembers. The judge went to Arizona and back recently without seeing or remembering a blessed thing, but he walked into the shop the other day with his head tilted back, muttering: "'A better bad habit of swearing, a better bad habit of swearing' than--than--what? That's what I want to know."

Steady, judge. What's up?"

"Nothing; 'a better bad habit of swearing?' Get me 'The Merchant of Venice.'" The play was brought to him. As he hurriedly turned the leaves of the book he muttered under his breath, "Talk to me about modern authors--any authors. Where is there anything like the description of Absalom:

"'From the sole of his foot even to the crown of his head there was no blemish in him.'

"Or this:

"'And Jacob served seven years for Rachel; and they seemed unto him but a few days for the love he had to her.'

"Oh, here it is," said the judge, and he read aloud Portia's words:

"'He hath a better bad habit of frowning than the Count Palatine.'

"And I would have sworn that it was 'swearing' and not 'frowning,'" declared Judge Osborne with a dreamy look on his face. "You see, I have been listening to a friend of mine talk, and his words reminded me of the quotation."

More Interesting Than Politics

Will somebody please tell the truth about the cow and her cud? In this country, when a cow suddenly grows pale and lethargic and ceases to do business with the water wagon, some old negro comes along and says, "She's lost her cud," and straightway he fastens a lot of greasy dish-rags to a hoe handle and rams the rags down the animal's throat. At once the cow resumes her complexion and her connection with the dairy, and, notwithstanding her hereditary loss of upper teeth, chews away as vigorously as a gum-girl. Is this fashion of loading a cow with old rags a superstition, or does her internal machinery really require occasional doses of red flannel? And when the old-time negroes--the only genuine cow doctors--die, what in the world will become of cows who are unfortunate enough to lose their cuds? The Old Man declares that this subject is more interesting to him than politics.

Col. Jones and His Witness

As a rule, women do not make good witnesses, by the way. They get nervous. This is especially true about women who know nothing about court-rooms except from reading newspapers, and imagine that lawyers earn their living by the merciless examination of witnesses. This fact was illustrated a year or so ago when the Summerrow-Baruch libel case was being tried. One of the witnesses was a Charlotte lady who happened to be in the Baruch store when Mrs. Summerrow received the alleged insults. The examination of the witness had been delayed for two days, and when she at length came to the stand she was visibly agitated. One understood her feeling. She imagined that some one intended to twist her up and force her to seem to tell an untruth. And, in spite of her fright, it could be seen that she had determined that she, a lone woman who was about to be badgered and browbeaten, should not be made to tell a lie. The examination was something like this:

"Madam," said Col. Hamilton C. Jones--a most courtly man--"please go ahead and tell what happened in the store. Tell it in your own way, and--"

"Now, Colonel Jones," interrupted the witness, "don't try to lay any trap for me. I came here to tell the truth and the truth I will tell, for--"

"But, madam," interrupted Col. Jones, "I assure you--"

"Colonel Jones, don't attempt to get me excited or mix me up. I don't know much about this case, and--"

"Madam," said the colonel a trifle sternly, "I have no wish to mix you up. All I want you to do is to give a plain recital of the facts. Now please go ahead and give your testimony. What took place in the store at the time you were there?"

"There you are, Colonel Jones, there you are trying to get me bothered," said the witness, who was tremendously excited. "If you will only let me alone--"

"But, madam, I am doing nothing to you. You are a witness in this case, and I must ask you to proceed with your evidence."

"Oh, I see you have laid a trap for me, Colonel Jones. I know I am only a woman and don't know anything about courts, but I would have thought, Colonel Jones--"

"But, madam--"

"I beg of you, Colonel Jones, not to persist in trying to make me tell a lie. As I said before--"

"Madam, I--"

"I came here as a witness who had no feeling one way or the other, and--"

"But, madam, I only want you to tell the truth, and I am doing nothing to disturb you."

"Oh, yes, you are, Colonel Jones--you know you are. I can plainly see that you have made up your mind to catch me in some way, and I must request you not to do that, Colonel Jones, for--"

"Stand aside, madam," said Colonel Jones, as he mopped the perspiration from his brow.

Down on French Art

As Mayor Brown sat in his private office Monday, reading a copy of Balzac in the original and occasionally reflecting on the possibilities of frog culture, a resident entered hurriedly and in an excited manner exclaimed:

"Voila!"

"Voila yourself," said the mayor pleasantly.

"Bon soir," said the visitor.

"Bon jour," observed the mayor.

"J'ai bonne cause," declared the visitor. "Out at the park auditorium they will play to-night 'Camille,' the naughty production of Alexander Dumas, fils. Oh, so improper, so shocking, so-er-en dishabille. So-er-vif! Cut it out, else we become corrupt."

"Nom de-- Voila! Garçon!" said the mayor; and then he sent for Chief of Police Irwin and instructed him to go out, tout frais fait, watch the "lady of the camelias" and corral all exposed portions of the French drama.

"Oui, oui," said the chief in the most excellent French. "Nous verrons," added the chief sternly. "Je main tiendrai le droit. Je suis pret," concluded the officer as he departed to gaze upon Camille.

An immense audience filled the auditorium. The fashionable folk who occupied seats paid ten cents per head. Those who stood up were charged nothing. Do you know "Camille"? Well, the play offers refinement and fascination in a setting of wickedness. Your interpretation of it is--as you like. The audience whooped its approval, and gave the first curtain calls of the season. "The Latta Park Stock Company played the thing as well as the Olga Nethersole company," proudly said Mr. F. D. Sampson, who manages the actor people. And there was no argument.

"If a woman comes out there on that stage without any--nous verrons," said the chief, tres chretiennement. "In other words, what I will do for Camille will be a plenty," observed the officer.

"Joli," said Officer Summerrow, from Newton, who also spoke most excellent French and is an authority on the Gallic school of art.

"Oui," said the chief scornfully.

The play proceeded, not merrily, of course, but to the entire satisfaction of the spectators, and the actors. The latter knew the object of the chief's visit, and watched him narrowly. To relieve the exciting, not to say morbid, tension of the play, they rigged a woman up for a vaudeville stunt which spelled more or less legs. And, for the sake of the law, they overdraped her until she was fashioned to widow's weeds. There could be no protest over any feature of the evening.

"I will return tout de suite--if not sooner," ejaculated the chief. "Every now and then I was sure somebody would bust over and do something downright wicked, but, voila, I was disappointed. Tracassarie all! Yet I am toujours pret to pull Camille or Lucille or Maud or Phyllis or just any of 'em."

"Voila," exclaimed the mayor when he heard the chief's report.

"Voila tout," said Chief Irwin.

"N' importe," remarked the fastidious resident.

"Good mornin', Carrie," said a voice from the Tombs.

Vive la Peruna!

The Afternoon Tea

"There's going to be an afternoon tea at my house," said a resident yesterday, "and I am going to leave home. An afternoon tea is a place where those present lose their digestion and those absent their reputation. I prefer to lose my reputation."

Corrected

"Forty naught, naught, one, please, central."

"You mean forty, aught, aught one?"

"Yes, thank you."

"You are welcome."

Alas!

Since the battle of Gettysburg, Col. H. C. Jones has shot quail, landed bass, and done everything else under a silk hat that had, somehow, become a part of himself. And now he wears a Panama. Displace a crown for tinsel--alas! alas!

CHAPTER XI
OBSERVATIONS ON LITERATURE

The Dime Novel

"The day of dime novels has almost passed," said an observant resident, "and the glory of the James boys, Wild Bill, Deadwood Dick and scores of other Western desperadoes is forgotten history. From the time of James Fenimore Cooper until ten or fifteen years ago this country was flooded with paper-backed, lurid tales which teemed with blood-spilling and hairbreadth escapes in every chapter, and handled the wonderful exploits of impossible New York detectives and the adventure and scalping parties on the plains with equal ease. The stories were the curse of nearly every school. Boys read them at home when they should have been studying their lessons, absorbed them stealthily during school hours, and discussed them at recess. The Frank Reade Company, the Beadles, and other cheap bookhouses made immense fortunes, and received a very large proportion of the pocket money of boys from Maine to Texas.

"But the dime novel doesn't pass muster with a generation that places a baseball player on a pedestal, nurses ping-pong pangs or kindred ailments, and splits its hair in the middle and goes to sit--around girl parties after fourteen years of age. Such boys are not interested in the noble yarn about Alkali Isaac's destroying an entire Indian village with his trusty bowie knife. They lack imagination, and don't care a hang for the details of the Custer fight, the fate of the last Mohican, or Old Sleuth's terrible fight with murderers in the Bowery. Modern boys, as a rule, don't read, and the younger men are little better. They hold up Sherlock Holmes as a criterion and laugh at the old-time detective tragedies; and they dabble in the emotional French school and sociological novels that prate dirty realism.

"Yes, you will see that the genus of youth has changed. Nowadays Fielding's Tom Jones doesn't even assume the dimensions of a ghost, and the vivid characters of Cooper, Marryat and their ilk are dying. And what boy knows Tom Sawyer or Huckleberry Finn? They teach physiology and Shylock in the schools, and the product cares for the two-step and not the deadly trail of the avenger. I'm sorry. The dime novel, taken at its worst, certainly kept a boy's mind active--made him think about something."

Books, Old and New

The booksellers usually have to go to the rear part of their stores or upstairs to get a book by an author whose reputation is justly fixed, but they're selling no end of red and blue and pink and green books that are written by unknown people. Blame the prevalent taste and not the booksellers. The classics sell in ten, twenty and thirty-cent shape. The characters in these are still used by our fathers and mothers for illustrative purposes, but we match reminiscences of cheap modern creatures who move vulgarly. The best-selling book is Rev. Tom Dixon's "The One Woman," and the literary quality of the author is something ghastly. The strongest novel of the year, in several continents, is Mrs. Humphry Ward's "Lady Rose's Daughter," a superbly written character-sketch and a morbid, unnatural book that a man wouldn't care for his sister to read. There's a Carnegie library down the street that has been in operation only a short time. Do you know what the majority of people--and especially the younger people--will take from there and read? The smelly, new books, of course. This is a cultured community, but the literary flavor is less of an inheritance than commercial prosperity. Who's to talk book lore worth hearing after the older generation passes away? Who's to replace these women who write Italian hands, argue the relative merits of the greatest poets, and can reproduce from memory Scott's best style? Who's to hold up a standard that understands--that rejects all that is not fine and strong and clean? A little while--and who will there be down here to mock the loud-hued books that reek with tawdry, rotten sentiment?

Oh, nobody. And it doesn't make any difference, does it? There is no money in the thing, anyway, and people can talk about something else. Of course they can . . . can talk of "pork and cabbages and kings" and the boll weevil and lots of things apart from literature. This protest, then? Why, don't take it seriously, please. You perceive that it filled a certain amount of space?

Voila tout!

The Speed Maniac

"The speed mania is the hoodoo of modern literature," said the observant resident. "You are always swearing at the new pink and green smelly books, but what else can you expect from authors who dictate to a stenographer? 'Wilhelm Meister' cost Goethe ten years of labor. Imagine a modern writer working ten months on a book! Woodrow Wilson, Thomas Nelson Page, Mark Twain and William Dean Howells are the only American writers who will live half a century hence; and Edgar Allan Poe is the only big literary light on this side of the water that will shine forever. In this made rush what chance is there to produce a great writer--who has time to think and prepare for writing? At the Baptist Convention here 'The Little Shepherd of Kingdom Come' was the only book that found encomiums, and the convention was at a high ebb of mentality. The truth of the matter is that there is no such thing nowadays as literary culture except among old people; and a hundred years from now people will not be caring to read anything except the newspapers."

Characters in Fiction

Dickens created handsome, likable fellows, but Steerforth is his only character that might have been labelled dangerous to woman. Scott's men won hearts with the same finesse that they won battles. Thackeray was an exact photographer and shows only everyday types. Bulwer Lytton's lordly men are mournfully pedantic and tiresome, Eugene Aram being a single exception. There is a subtle fascination about the Richard Feverel of George Meredith; but the most striking figure of the English school of fiction is John Rochester in Jane Eyre. He is a man--all man; fine, faulty, stern, tender, humorous, intense. Any one who reads Jane Eyre must come under the influence of John Rochester. His was a presence that must have been felt in any room; he had all the simple elements that appeal to both women and men. In all fiction he is the most vivid, pulsing figure.

Among present-day writers there are only three who have the sure art of portraying fascinating men--Henry Seton Merriman, Anthony Hope and

Richard Harding Davis. This assertion comes from one who reckons the three writers below first class, but their men are clearly drawn and are the kind of men that would fascinate women. Kipling has the queer power of making one understand how his men could chain and hold forever one woman--but only one woman.

Apart from the characters of Richard Harding Davis, the men in the American school of fiction make no particular impression on the reader. They are too unnatural. Look back upon all the American books you have read and you are not apt to recall a single lover who is worth the name. What one is fascinating? Where is a single one that is half so attractive as the idle, careless Van Bibber men? Where is one whose charm is proved by his creator?

But the writer did not intend to be led into the discussion of a subject that permits unlimited room for difference of opinion. In brief space he has had latitude from St. Elmo to Launcelot, and has merely voiced personal preference. Thoughts of the latter-day men who break up happy homes was the real reason for this rumination, anyway. And they don't do it; that's the blunt reply to The Gazette. In the smoking car you have had men who wore loud ties, and hats on the back of their heads, sit down beside you and tell you about the wreckage they had created by their contact with the eternal feminine. They would have led you to believe that whenever they entered a village young women followed them just as the children followed the Pied Piper of Hamelin. These fellows and the cads who stand in hotel lobbies or in the drinking rooms of clubs and blow about their prowess with women--they are all little rough fools who would jar the sensibilities of a washerwoman. These reputed, or admitted, heart-breakers--they don't really do any business, to put it crudely. The modern man, any way you take him, is not built for a fascinator. He is a business machine whose clothes are not pretty, whose muscles are apt to be flabby, and who converses with a woman just as he dictates to a typewriter. If he wins one woman he is lucky; if he fascinates two, the world holds up its hands and sees not the fluke that is, but the fascination that exists in the imagination. Any man can understand why any other man can fall in love with almost any woman, but no man can understand why any woman should fall in love with any man. Which suggests that the writer may not be altogether unprejudiced.

Favorite Passages

The judge was not prepared to say what he thought was the finest or most expressive sentence in literature. Are you? It is an interesting matter to puzzle over. For some reason Victor Hugo's characterization of Napoleon has always impressed the writer more than anything he ever read:

"The mighty somnambulist of a vanished dream," said the French author in speaking of Napoleon after the battle of Waterloo.

The best description of anger is in "Hiawatha":

"And his heart was hot within him;

Like a burning coal his heart was."

Going to the other extreme, Tennyson was probably happiest in a tender couplet-picture of the effect of love. Some one asked him once what he liked best in all the things he had written. He picked up a pen and wrote:

"Love took up the harp of life and smote on all the chords with might, Smote the chord of self, that, trembling, passed in music out of sight."

Apropos of Biblical quotations, did you ever see anything humorous in the Bible? If you haven't, you read the history of Jacob until you come to the place where it says:

"And Jacob kissed Rachel, and lifted up his voice and wept."

That sentence presents the funniest picture ever. Just imagine a man walking up to a strange woman, kissing her on the mouth, and then throwing back his head and bursting into tears. What an orful chump Jacob must have seemed to Rachel!

"Recessional" in Mitchell County

"Kipling reached Mitchell County in 1898--that is, his 'Recessional' arrived there that year," said a visitor in the city. "A certain newspaper in this State kept ringing the changes on the thing and the lawyers over in the mountains got hold of the poem. They worked it to sensational advantage, and for four successive terms of court every lawyer who went before a Bakersville jury was loaded with the 'Recessional.' You know, nobody in the world can speak like those mountain lawyers who roll back their cuffs over the sleeves of their long frock coats, and sweat, and talk at the top of their voices. They liked Kipling, and on a quiet day you could hear 'em screaming 'Lord God of Hosts!' for a mile, while the jurors chewed tobacco and wept. The iteration of 'Lest we forget' in a big voice has won many a verdict in a blockading case, and the impressive conclusion of a peroration with 'Our far-flung battle line' saved the day in a murder trial. Kipling became the most popular man in Mitchell, and the attorney who made the most effective recitation of the 'Recessional' was generally a winner. Matters came to such a pass, finally, that Kipling's influence was felt even in little ejection cases. The situation was so serious that the judges decided that a single 'Lest we forget' would be held as contempt of court. This ended the reign of Kipling, which will be memorable in the annals of Mitchell."

The Cowboy in Fiction

Out on these terrible western-flavored plays that are forever dragging coarse-mannered men with pistols and crude speech into drawing rooms and marrying them to women who use Bostonesey words and wear resplendent gowns. The Virginian in Owen Wister's book was all right; but the slow-talking Westerner with his eternal prate about "Mavericks" and his ridiculously loving heart is getting to be offly tiresome. It is a pity that Tim Murphy has such an absurd character to impersonate. The cowboy is being overdone--exalted too much. He is so sweet and childish and tries so hard to keep from eating up other people that he ought to fly in with wings strapped to him--if he could only manage to conceal his pistols for a minute or so. The cowboy plays and these ghastly things that picture domestic scenes in New

England don't seem to go down here, somehow or other. Even the London society plays are more popular. In these everybody is deliciously and consistently wicked, and no wild Indian types mar harmony by trying to do refined stunts. The cowboys are the limit.

"The Age of Charm"

In an article in Ainslee's Magazine Miss Geraldine Bonner discusses "The Age of Charm" in women, and gives a very interesting running summary of the ages of the famous women in fiction and history. Sir Walter Scott's heroines were sixteen or seventeen years old; those of Thackeray and Dickens twenty. Jane Eyre was only nineteen years of age, "an error in art for which the fashion of the day is responsible." Juliet, the only heroine in Shakespeare whose age is given, was fourteen years old. Balzac surprised the world by introducing to it still fresh and bewitching women of thirty. Diane de Poicters and Madame de Maintenon were forty; and "the women of the salons and the Revolution continued these traditions of an irresistible fascination at the age of autumnal maturity." Anne Boleyn was twenty-four years old. Stella was loved best by Dean Swift when she was nearly forty. Venus de Milo was thirty-two, and Thackeray is the expert authority who declares that thirty-two is the age when a woman is in her perfect moment of full bloom. Cleopatra was thirty-eight when she and Antony "kissed away kingdoms"; and Helen of Troy was nearly forty when Paris was smitten with her beauty.

Wagner's "Simple Life"

There are a number of the best critics who consider "The Simple Life," by Charles Wagner, the strongest of the new books that are having a large sale at the present time. The purpose of the book is attractive enough surely. It is a "plea for simplicity in life--for simple thoughts, simple words, simple needs, simple beauty." There is such a nauseating amount of the other sort of thing. Yet pretence never deceived anybody. The real heart of the man shows in spite of himself. That is sad, and sometimes exposes a hypocrite. Brains are not rated for more than they are worth, and thus is given continual opportunity to laugh at pretenders. Everybody who mixes with the world is estimated at a true valuation. Everybody who isn't simple is a fool. There are no bounds to the application of the text. It demands daily humility for one's self and charity for one's neighbor. One person in a thousand wants a simple life, and everybody bows before it in admiration. Who do you know that is simple, really simple--leads a simple life? And who is happy that isn't simple--doesn't lead a simple life? The questions are apart from the book-- just suggested by the title. But who does care for simple words, simple thoughts, simple beauty? Nowadays childhood, going into maturity, gets a training that fits it to give the wrong sort of reply.

Magic

"In the Forest of Arden," a children's story that Mrs. Margaret Busbee Shipp has been writing for The Observer, is very sweet and human. It shows genuine children; breathes a charming, natural prattle. It lacked only in one point. In the story nobody said to nobody else, "One time there was a bear." Just those words were necessary, and the child who has not quivered in anticipation at the darksome sound of the sentence has missed one of the greatest pleasures. Cluster little ones at your knee and speak on fairies and sprites and nymphs and godmothers and hobgoblins, and they will desert you in the middle of your narrative at the cry of "One time there was a bear." It is not permissible to say, "In the dear, dead days of long ago there resided a bear," or anything like that. You must be very solemn and dignified and say just, "One time there was a bear." Any sort of a story will be satisfactory after this beautiful prelude. But you needn't try to win success by saying "One time there was a lion," or "One time there was a elerphunt." No, no--you will be merely wasting your time. "One time there was a bear!" In the distant ages some great philosopher, longing to bring a common blessing to all mankind, must have created that marvellous utterance. It will bring a thrill of ecstacy to the boy, and it makes the little woman nestle closer and closer to you, confidingly, humorously, expectantly. If the Pied Piper of Hamelin had only known what to say he needn't have blown on his flute. . . . "One time there was a bear!"

"The Right of Way"

"The Right of Way," the best thing that has ever been written by Mr. Gilbert Parker, and the strongest novel that has been published in years, has become an all-absorbing topic of local literary discussion. In a small town in the western part of this State the book clubs dropped Balzac and Maeterlinck recently and fell to warring as to whether or not "The Right of Way" is immoral. The conflict is still on. The truth is that the book is as clean as cleanness except, perchance, one reads it looking for--trouble. It is quite beautiful and strong and artistic.

"The Little Shepherd of Kingdom Come"

"The Little Shepherd of Kingdom Come," by John Fox, Jr., is having a larger sale than any of the new books displayed by the local bookstores. It is well written and gives a fascinating picture of life in Kentucky. Yet in holding up as a hero a Southern man who fought for the Union side, through conscientious motive, the book essays a difficult task. That sort of exploit was not admired or interesting in real life. As the basis for a novel it is rather unsafe; for the author and the reader will have different opinions of the real character of the hero. Still, the book is very readable. The more one sees of the other modern books the more he likes "The Virginian," the best novel that has been written in America in many years.

A Thought from Stevenson

Even on Sunday night, when the whole world has returned from preaching and is filled with spiritual exhortation, it may not be out of place to think on the words of "A Task," written by Robert Louis Stevenson. They are for living purposes only and read:

"To be honest, to be kind, to earn a little and to spend a little less, to make upon the whole a family happier for his presence, to renounce when that shall be necessary and not be embittered, to keep a few friends, but these without capitulation, above all, on the same grim condition, to keep friends with himself--here is a task for all that a man has of fortitude and delicacy."

CHAPTER XII
IDEALS OF WRITING AND SPEAKING

The Simple Style

To have a thing to tell and to tell it--that is the spirit of modern writing. Time was when the world found sheer fascination in voluminous and bitter controversy as to how many angels could stand on the point of a needle, and the thought of putting the vernacular or plain speech in books was horrifying. Only now and then, through many ages, did a great, simple light shine. Most brains were beclouded with ponderous phrases. There was a rumbling in the head and words poured on paper with the limitless ease of a schoolboy's commas. To write grandly, mystically, transcendentally--that was the old-time idea. Judged by present standards, this was a waste of raw material and quite boring. The classics that live and are best known are strongest in simplicity, in the easy telling of a thing. The venerable johnnies who died in literature used a million words too many.

And the easiest writing is the hardest writing. Which is a compliment to the new school, whose demand is to trim to the briefest statement of truth or opinion. Maybe the principle is too businesslike for beauty, but it gains in other respects. Blackstone knew the law, but one of the New York Sun's cracks could take any of Blackstone's volumes, rewrite it in half size, and never lose an argument or fact. The newspaper theory is to nail the dynamic point in the first paragraph, to then swing to your rhetorical introduction, development and conclusion, and to play up your stuff so that you may hold interest till the last line is read. Style and clean diction are not forgotten, but writing for writing's sake is the unforgivable crime. With such a criterion it is small wonder that the new school scorns the methods of the past.

"I have always had one idea in writing an editorial," said one of the best-known Southern editors to the writer. "I have in mind a man in the middle of a crowd and I want to brush aside everything and reach him, hold him as quickly as possible. The man represents the main point that I wish to make, and I feel hampered till I have clinched him." 'Tis the same idea, you see. No matter what the subject may be, writing that has a thing to tell and tells it without ever losing sight of a purpose--why, that writing commands attention and is durable.

Ideas are incidental, or unnecessary. Referring to an article written by a rather important personage in a neighboring town, a resident said in serious pride: "He wrote so fine that but very few people could understand him." Yet in the name of art and common sense the communication in question should have been reduced from one thousand to one hundred words. It was all just fine writing--the result of half-education, conceit and an ear for music. Strong, sure, eloquent speech is most beautiful. It is clothed fine, maybe, but is ruthlessly direct in its splendor. It is most often the clear, terse thought from the mind of a gentleman; is independent in strength, and needs no word trickery. Editor Marshall, of the Gastonia Gazette, is always talking about some man who writes iceberg English--stuff that shivers one with its cool incisiveness, and Mr. Marshall very wisely holds up this literature as his model. Yet most writers reach out for fine writin' and will be sophomores to the end of their days; being unmindful of the fact that the simplest and best, as well as the hardest, way of word-making consists in the selection of short, pungent Saxon sentences.

The increased number of North Carolinians who indulge in foreign travel has, somehow, resulted in few personal lectures on the old country. There seems to be an impression that a three-months' journey on the Continent is not necessarily followed by either expert or interesting information, and a denizen with hayseed in his hair has been known to yawn over a garrulous account of the wickedness of Paree.

The man who has a mind to see things and knows how to tell them is the only person who has an appreciative audience. He may be fresh from St. Petersburg or he may come from Paw Creek, but if he understands his fellow-man and the quality of human interest his observations will command attention anywhere. Nine-tenths of the world talks incessantly, but the one-tenth doesn't listen one-tenth of the time. A bit of humor picked up in a cornfield may make all mankind laugh, or the seeing of pathos in the death of a yellow dog in the back country may cause thousands to weep, but a suit case tagged by half a dozen foreign capitals is no guarantee that the owner will not wag his tongue in vain speech and boredom. Anybody can write and anybody can talk, but it is a herculean task to hold anybody's attention for five minutes."

Once more the protest comes against those writers who insist upon refusing to allow a dead man to die. People who write obituary notices on this subject are not expected to be perfectly clear as to expression; but one shudders over the way men on the State press murder adjectives, adverbs and long, stout clauses in efforts to get around a succinct statement of facts. Why? Is there a word in the English language that is half as strong as--dead? He is dead. Can you write anything more stately or eloquent than that sentence? Yet even papers like The New Orleans Times-Democrat ramble rhetorical miles out of the way to keep from using the word. You see it: "He has passed into the unknown," or "He has entered sweetly into rest," or "The spirit winged its flight." These expressions are all right in their place, but they become distasteful when a newspaper man, who is supposed to nail his essential facts in his first paragraph, uses them with a weepily eloquent idea of avoiding a word that touches heaven with its sublime strength. "Into the night--into the light!" Death! Dead! God and eternity are in the word. And it is a simple, fair word, opposing unkind discrimination and offering dignity above final democracy.

A Bit of Rhetoric

A specimen of Mr. Henry Blount's rhetoric, printed in this paper a week or so ago, has attracted a good deal of attention. In one sentence, which was exactly a quarter of a column long in actuality and heaven high in sentiment, Mr. Blount lassoed all the biggest descriptive adjectives and more metaphors than the ordinary writer would use in a year. His climax, it may be remembered, pictured, in a majestic style, a moth that had wiped a bitter tear from its eye and had decided that it would not fix a "corroding fang." It must be grand to be able to write like that. In his entire literary career Mr. Blount never said or thought anything that he could relate in Anglo-Saxon, and, without a bit of effort, he sees the stars singing together as the peroration to a dog fight and a sun-kissed goddess instead of a cross-eyed blonde. In all his years of newspaper work Mr. Blount recognized nothing as trivial or prosaic, and always, when he speaks, there comes that steady flow of gurgling, rhythmic words, not to be likened to the language of any other man that ever lived. He is a genius--a happy genius, though one may differ with him about rhetorical qualities and quantities. For Henry Blount is ever on the Alps, and at breakfast he wears a mood that may seldom bless the ordinary man, making him wish to bare his head under the beauty of the starlit sky or humble himself reverentially in the presence of Nature's perfection.

The College Graduate

"Once more the graduates are leaving college and are going out to face the world," said the observant man, "and I am wondering which of the boys will try to learn and which will try to teach--which will succeed and which will fail. I speak of learning and teaching in the larger, untechnical sense. I have seen valedictorians who went out with communicative but unreceptive minds to teach things to the world. They now have charge of schools at forty dollars a month. I have seen boys who made second-year math. by a fluke, and who won college reputation only as athletes. They walked into sterner living with a keen wish to absorb and learn, and as the years passed they came to the intellectual life. A college education is only the beginning of things, and it has ruined a man when it sent him out as a self-constituted tutor to the rest of mankind. You recognize that type the instant you see it. It includes young men, middle-aged men and old men, and none of them has any capacity for growth. The habit of trying to teach or tell things to the world is incurable, and it is too apt to begin at college. It will spoil the lawyer, the politician--injure any man in public or private life. It will make a man the dictator at a family dinner table, the spokesman for every crowd on the streets, and it will close his ears to the instruction that he should receive from his fellow man every day that he lives. Mark the man who listens and thinks, and the man who thinks he knows it all and talks without listening. The talkers are in the majority in the world, but the listeners--the learners--rule the world."

Use of Words

A man writes by the light that the Lord has given him: and the Comment Man says "unnice" and "unsweet," because he likes the sense and sound of the words. Looking for his good-natured critic, he sees the visage of Mr. Henry A. Page, of Aberdeen, a man whose opinion on any subject must challenge attention. But, seriously, Mr. Page, what is the matter with "unsweet"? Lord Bacon loved the word, and in his "Essay on Death"--a model for all the ages--he says:

"But I consent with Caesar, that the suddenest passage is the easiest, and there is nothing more awakens our resolve and readiness to die than the quieted conscience, strengthened with opinion that we shall be well spoken of upon earth by those that are just and of the family of virtue; the opposite whereof is a fury to man, and makes even life unsweet." Man, where can you find anything quainter or finer than this? "Makes even life unsweet"--can't you understand that?

Col. Al. Fairbrother, editor of Everything, campions the word anent, and says it is a smooth and juicy word. That's a matter of taste. But you never heard any one use the word in conversation, or pronounce it easily or naturally. It is one of the few old Saxon or Scotch words that lack in strength and euphony. But a man can't be dogmatic about this matter. He likes certain words and he doesn't like certain words; that is all. And the writer abominates anent and alas and lovely. Col. Fairbrother remembers that a correspondent once "jumped astride the comment man" for using the word unnice. He did. It was Henry Page, who in the same breath held up the word nasty as a desirable expression for euphemistic parlance. There was a fierce little row, and after it was all over the mind of the comment man wasn't changed in the least. He likes unnice and he likes unsweet; but he hasn't written either of the words since he had the mix-up with Henry Page. He thinks them a lot, however; thinks that anent is unsweet, and that both you and Henry Page, Col. Fairbrother, have unnice, cranky ideas about "word-slinging," to borrow a term that you exercise in your sublimest peroration. But man's a sensitive thing, after all, and he can be broken from using any words except sweet words. The Old Man says that once the New Orleans Times-Democrat referred to something and then added that it was up to the Charlotte Observer to say: "You ought to be ashamed of yourself." It occurred to him then that nearly all his journalistic life he had been writing at one time and another, "You ought to be ashamed of yourself"--jestfully, of course. His pet phrase, just like unnice and unsweet, is held in abeyance these days. But you are incorrigible, Colonel Fairbrother. If it has occurred to your subtle mind that anent is a nice, poetical word, you'll go on trying to create lockjaw with it for the balance of your days. Nothing short of a club could ever persuade you from riding your own outlandish, devilish words.

The Inexpressible

If a strong, clear-headed man were to speak according to the heart that is in him--tell the throbbing history of a soul--the world would stop and listen. When he comes to paint the sorrow of death he must not expose his own anguish as he stood at the bier, but he delves into his imagination for another man, and pictures, most often, a suffering that is not real. And who, in writing a love story, would dare display the brooding sweetness of a personal experience? The greatest writers are those who understand the things about them and can tell these things. But the simple inner history --or confession-- of any one of half the people one knows might be more sensational than all the books ever written.

As the jester jests, a man in the club upstairs is playing the Intermezzo on a muffled piano, and the notes steal down to mock laughter. Music and the mood stay the hand that would be facetious. Pierrot was unmirthful awhile. There's no need, or scant wish, in the telling, but . . . music--certain tender notes--clutch and hold one. There's a tremulousness of strength, a fullness, a touch of completeness--indescribable. And words are helpless, hopeless. To write them as one felt --ay, it is impossible. To feel, to be moved till there's a gulp in the throat, to be swayed by an emotion till life is quickened to the utmost and to be able to write then --then. . . . No. 'Tis not given to do. So is pathos.

Often a newspaper cannot touch more than the surface life, and books handle vital personal episodes only by holding up puppets to play with. The only thing really worth while studying is a living human being who sins, or suffers, or exults, or loves, or is disgraced, or perishes--all in our sight or within our knowledge. All we see or think about, more than all we know we speak about, and then we may write about only that which is too uninteresting to talk about, or too notorious for silence. The thought has passed beyond things scandalous, and considers the thousand and one fascinating little human incidents that occur in the daily life, and must be told in lip service and not by a pen. They are ever seeable to a newspaper man, but for use in his craft they are ever denied him. He stands in the dry-as-dust path or rut and must take the things that come, while his heart aches to revel in the near-by field which is filled with people and a prattle that is not great, but humanly intimate, and strong enough to make all mankind stop and listen. The writer would like to write one book--not a sociological or historical novel, but a book that revealed the naked, inner truth in the life and living of a man or woman--almost any man or woman, and if he could do this honestly and accurately he would be content, knowing that he had done a deed that was new under the sun. Do you understand the fierce temptation to write with gloves off--to go behind the mocking outwardness and paint a picture in warm, soft colors that would betray the secret soul of childhood, the weakness and the strength of youth's passion, the sweetness and pitifulness of old age, the mask of hypocrisy, and faces, not as one pretends to see them, but as one really sees them? But the want is useless, for--

A man up in the club is playing Gottschalk's "Last Hope," and the music is bothersome to another man who is trying to write nonsense. The man in the club is operating a Cecilian that is tacked on to a piano, and he probably has his coat off and is looking no more sentimental than a fish, but heard from this distance the music is as tender and beautiful as it was intended to be. It belongs to the kind of music that makes one think things that he can't write about, or it creates a misty, dreamy realm that is filled with wet violets and a certain kind of eyes. A curse on the lameness of a pen! A man is forever wanting to write about things that he doesn't want to write about, or else he is palsied in his efforts to deduce interest from practical things. To write one paragraph on a level with the simple spirit of that music--to stand under the heavens and speak fitting majesty in a sentence--to describe the look on a mother's face as she touches a nestling infant. . . . Aye, the impossible is asked! The big, surging things in us are dumb. Every living man has been glorified by something that stood for inspiration--by some leap of blood that quickened him to the fulness of living and appreciation--and silenced him. Oh, the fretting is idle. Nordica sang and everybody said 'twas beautiful. How beautiful--the effect of the song? And there was silence while eyes glowed feverishly. Baffled? That's it. The paper said the song was beautiful. So! Miss Pansy Blossom, who is coming over here next week to visit Miss Priscilla Smith, is also beautiful, they say. The foolish idea of trying to say anything with words!

Art of Story Telling

The telling of this little incident is additional proof to the writer that the effect of some funny situations cannot be conveyed in words. Words are bleak, unmeaning things at times. A little while ago a man came to this office and he was laughing so he could hardly speak. Eventually he said between hysterics:

"Funniest thing I ever heard happened down yonder to-night. Oh, it's too good to keep, and it will make the best newspaper story in the world."

"What is it?"

"As soon as I can get my breath I'll write it for you," he replied.

After a while he wiped the laughter-tears from his eyes, reached for some paper, sharpened a pencil as he tittered, and began to write. He wrote a line or two on half a dozen sheets of paper and crumpled 'em up and chucked 'em in the waste basket. Sharpening his pencil again, he scrawled a couple of lines, and then rested his head on his hand and thoughtfully shaded the letters he had already made. The gradual change in his expression was interesting. At first his face beamed, then he condescended to smile only occasionally, and finally he was quite serious. An hour passed and he sat there with his eyes sort of protruding and cold perspiration on his forehead. The muse wouldn't work. He had not written half a page, but his fingers were gripped as if he suffered from paralysis. The humor simply refused to leak onto the paper. The mental strain grew terrible to witness. Finally he reached for his hat, walked to the door, and in parting said:

"Say, the darned thing is not half as funny as I thought it was."

The joke was never told.

"Commend me to a man who can tell a story without superfluous words or gestures," remarked a clever Charlotte man. "The telling of nine stories out of ten is hurt by wild waving of hands and arms or the interjection of words that are top-weights for the tale. Dr. Buttrick, the secretary of the General Educational Board, is the first exception to the rule that I have met in a long time. I saw him at the banquet the other night lay his hand on his fork, and, speaking for ten minutes, he never made a movement or grimace. The simple selection and pronunciation of his words attracted and held the attention of everybody around him. This was the perfection of story telling--an art that is almost forgotten."

Modern Oratory

How a phrase rings and throws the mind off at a tangent. Was it not Ingersoll who, in speaking of his brother's death, said:

"He has gone into the night--into the light."

What antithesis! It is simple Saxon sayings like this that live. Words that are the vernacular of the people show the strength and the polish of the greatest minds. If "damn" had three syllables mankind wouldn't swear.

Modern oratory searches for ideas after high words and euphony--is a clumsily arranged tale told by sound and gestures. Cicero in his speech against Cataline, and Mr. Walter Page in his address here the other night before the educational conference, expressed their meaning in clear, incisive words, but a majority of other speakers have been confusing the seven hills of Rome with any subject at issue. Twentieth-century audiences are as badly persecuted as the early Christians.

Bad Taste

Down in the legislative halls in Raleigh they're still talking about Senator Vance. Too much praise may not be said of that statesman and simple gentleman, but there is something unnice in the way his name is invoked on the smallest pretext. In many legislatures it has been customary for orators, no matter whether they wished a no-fence law or a bill for the relief of a crossroads, to get up and violently swear, honestly and by patriotism, by the memory of that immortal leader. The name of Vance, dragged into a speech as a part of personal eulogy, and flaunted in shocking bad taste, is heard too often on the political stumps in all parts of this State. Oh, this screaming, nauseous sentiment that reeks with prate of deity, or a father's grave, or the profane use of the name of a dead leader like Vance, whose fine scorn would have blasted such methods!

Simplicity in the Pulpit

The world is full of preachers who are splendidly educated and who get about seven hundred dollars a year for preaching. They are consecrated men who pore over the Scripture and use long Greek and Hebrew quotations with the greatest ease and constancy. As they grow older they increase in learning, but their salary remains about the same. A minister like Dr. Vance, of Newark, N. J., who gets six thousand dollars a year, is worth studying. What do they pay him all that money for? Why does he command so much more wages than nine-tenths of the other ministers? This thought was in the mind of one person, at least, who listened to Dr. Vance last night at the Second Presbyterian church. Dr. Vance's personality is pleasant enough, but he is not particularly magnetic. He has an ordinary voice. He preaches less than half an hour. Yet when he concludes a sermon one understands, without wonderment, why he commands a big price. He is unusual because he is perfectly simple. He indulges in no flowers, no hazy metaphysical language. He has a thing to say and he says it in Anglo-Saxon. He indulges in no hackneyed rhetorical climaxes. He is as plain as an old shoe; and his eloquence is in his earnestness. Any child can understand him, it was said, of course. His talk has the rhetorical sound of Robinson Crusoe in words of one syllable. His secret is nothing else but simplicity; and his experience ought to be an invaluable lesson to all those who speak for good effect or pay.

Affectation in Speech

Pahst and lahst and cahn't are the birthright of the Britishers, Bostonians and a few Virginians, but are to be marked as boomerangs when handled by those of alien breed. Speech and refined table manners are the essentials by which all men are judged. In the pride of his social heart one may consistently wear an elegant oyster harpoon as a watch guard, but when he learns to dahnce at adult age he borrows trouble which he cannot conceal. The theft of the longish "a" seems to be the peculiar prerogative of young women, who usually say "i-ther" and "nee-ther." It is the construction of a pitfall to introduce the broad a into fair speech--such being rare by a token of pity. And to hamper an I-have-saw and he-taken lingo with a penchant for dahncing is a thing to make the gods weep bitterly. Now, it was only a little while ago at a local card party that The Lady, with a graceful wave of her willowy neck, said:

"Cahn't-eu see that it was your lahst chawnce and you orter tuck the trick?"

Stump-speaking to the Lord

Dr. J. William Jones, chaplain general of the United Confederate Veterans, who is to lecture at the Presbyterian College auditorium, in this city, next Thursday night, on "Stonewall Jackson as a Soldier," will receive a warm welcome here. Before an immense audience in Charlotte, several weeks ago, Dr. Jones spoke of "The Christian Character of Jackson," and, holding close to his theme, he was most impressive and interesting. After dwelling at length on the fervor and simplicity of Jackson's prayers, Dr. Jones said:

"Jackson made no stump-speeches to the Lord."

And every person in the vast audience knew exactly what the speaker meant. What a difference there is between the quiet earnestness of the old-time man of God and the wordy bill of particulars that is so frequently heard in sophomoric and classic effusions! It must be no easy thing to learn to pray in public, but the glibness and the combinations of high-sounding phrases that come with practice are sometimes harder--for the congregation.

Stump-speaking in prayer is rather more intolerable than the absurdity that comes from ignorance or confusion. The laugh-provoking qualities of some prayers are admitted even by the best of ministers, who would fail to find mirth in the utterance of the fashionable Boston clergyman of whom it was said "he offered up the most eloquent prayer that was ever addressed to a Boston audience," but would be irresistibly amused at the stumbling, ludicrous petition of an honest, Christian soul. The declaration of the gentleman who was unable to stop the approach of the bear by prayer has record in profane history, but stories funnier than this and strictly within prayer-meeting limits may be told by almost every minister. Squire Calton Giles, of Burke County, sometime high church officer and local exhorter, requested merciful consideration for a good brother who lived two miles up the river on the Walton place close to the fish trap. He was always that specific. His pastor kept smile from his face; petitioned without reference to the fish trap and in rhetorical, flowery phrase that the congregation, at least, had to take on trust. The point to this dissertation--if point be allowed by courtesy--is directed, in a measure, at a clergyman in this city, who told gleefully of the break of a church officer in a prayer meeting, and yet the same preacher on the following Sunday night, used, in a brief petition, the words "circumambient," "iridescent" and "corollary." Which the Boston audience would have appreciated soberly.

But stump-speaking be barred

CHAPTER XIII
MUSIC AND DRAMA

"Melisse" in Morganton

Except in "Melisse," which was played in three night stands in Morganton and other small towns in the western part of the State fifteen or twenty years ago, never was such a histrionic success. Home talent in Morganton had been parading dukes and duchesses in ancestral wedding garments for many moons, but no real, live theatrical company had appeared in the hamlet since Mr. Wister Tate was mayor. Which was a long time. The players did about on the town hall stage behind a red curtain, which was worked on a big twine string. Their scenery looked like pictures in the barber shop, but they played a play that thrilled the entire population. It was related that Mr. John Happoldt, who had been to New York, had said that "Melisse" was as fine as anything he had ever seen there, and everybody frowned at Mr. Zach Corpening, who had been to New Orleans and who yawned and left the house during the first act. The next day people gathered in groups on the streets and rehearsed, with pantomime effect, the beautiful utterances of Melisse and her cowboy lover. The little town hall was transformed to a place beautiful, and when the cowboy stood full under the large kerosene lamp and drew two pistols and shouted at the top of his voice, "I will avenge her with me life," or something like that, everybody just riz right up and made the welkin ring. "Melisse" marked the first injection of modern dramatic art into the village, and after that nobody was particularly interested when somebody that everybody knew wore a familiar suit of Sunday clothes and cried, "Wilt be mine, Lady Pauline?" The cowboy marked an epoch. Melisse inspired fevered dreams. The curtain had disclosed a new world. Youth saw blissfully and found no flaw. Dear, dear Melisse!

The theme is not for fun-making. There is no happiness in learning to know how to criticise. 'Tis a fault that comes with age. It must come by a token of weariness. A man looks back at his childhood, remembers what the child's eyes saw, and, maybe, laughs at the remembrance, and yet he sighs for the rare pleasure that was before disillusionment came. "Manhood," some one said, "is but the dusty wareroom where are stored life's broken dreams." It isn't that bad, but it teaches a man too much knowledge that is not sweet, while never fully guarding him against the errors of inexperience. To have kept the simple, light heart that found peace and enjoyment in the littlest things--aye, that would be something. One should weep now over Melisse and her wondrous cowboy. Who found content after he was introduced to the real Santa Claus?

The Theatre and the Public

Charlotte theatre-goers have demonstrated the fact that they will put up any amount of money to see a good show, but they will not patronize a poor performance unless they are deceived into thinking it is good. The three star attractions that played here last week made almost as much money in Charlotte as they made in towns like Atlanta and Richmond, which are several times larger than this city; and all other first-class shows that have been here this season have had flattering audiences. The theatrical criterion here is high, though not exacting. It is almost a proverb to say that when Charlotte people leave home they go to New York; and this is mentioned to indicate that there is here a prevalent, though not overweening, knowledge of what is worth while in the play-acting world. Poor plays are treated mercilessly here, and the newspaper that treats them mercifully is apt to be mocked by its patrons or friends. Everybody looks uncritically upon the ten, twenty and thirty cent productions, but beyond that--when the orchestra seats stand at $1.50--there is a keen-eyed demand that the people on the stage act up to their pretensions, and if they don't they get a roast that lives for a long time and a long ways. A bum show makes a very sad mistake in coming here.

The only trouble with the Gordon-Shay Company is that it tried to do what it couldn't do and will never be able to do. Apart from the Calve and Melba contingent, thousands try to sing grand opera, but the individual can count the successes that he has witnessed on the fingers of one hand. They are very seldom seen here, though, by a grim token, a new voice periodically walks on the stage in evening clothes and marks failure in striving for unattainable notes. This refers to the ultra-classical music--to the bird that can't sing and will try to sing beyond its power or training. This side of the goal fixed by a few Grand Artists there is such a beautiful world of music and melody, and why is it that the people who can play in it prettily so often spoil themselves and the pleasure of others by overstepping bounds and mocking an art that punishes all mockery so cruelly?

A Battle Royal

There was a battle royal last night between the Italian with his street piano and the Rentfrow Company's band.

The Italian came here six or seven days ago and had the run of the place undisturbed for several days. At all hours of the day he could be heard grinding out music, while the little green bird in the cage at the top of his piano did a lucrative business in telling fortunes. The curious gave the bird's master ten cents, and then the bird selected, with its bill, yellow and red pamphlet forecasts, which informed a man that he would have a severe experience but he would overcome it and live happily to the age of seventy; and a woman that she must not be downhearted if her first marriage resulted unsatisfactorily--that she would outlive it and make others.

The Italian was out of town Monday and in his absence the Rentfrow Company, with its band, arrived. The Italian did the usual amount of business yesterday morning and evening, without the first sound of competition; but as the piano paused in front of the Central Hotel last night about eight o'clock and unwound the strains of "The Holy City," there was a sudden rude, discordant jar as the band stepped in front of the opera house a block away and began to enliven the atmosphere with a rag-time tune. The trick bird woke up and gasped in astonishment. The Roman muttered "Can these things be?" and ordered force pressure on "The Holy City." But the rag-time became louder and livelier, and the adherents of the musical Roman began to gradually desert him for coon-song airs. The little green bird grew greener with rage.

The gentleman from Italy recognized that his battery was firing too slowly and that he must charge in the face of the rapid-fire brass guns. His courage rose, and, with his eye in fine frenzy rolling, he got into the shafts of the rolling box and charged down the street to fight a rear-guard action. Half a block down he stopped, unlimbered, caught the revolving crank, and fired into the enemy's broadsides with heavy bars of "The Georgia Camp-meeting." There was a momentary demoralization among the brass horns, but they rallied and replied with deadly clog-dance artillery. The notes met in mid-air and screamed and wrestled and fell all over the shop; and the little green bird gave a throaty chirrup of excitement.

The crowd paused, uncertain, and the battle was in doubt. The Rentfrow ammunition was exhausted for a minute, and the wanderer from the Italian coast once more slipped the cog to "The Holy City"--a war hymn in slow time. Then the band found another coon song which almost submerged the pious craft. Yet once more Italian bravery asserted itself, and, travelling at full speed, the piano made a last stand in front of the Buford. Though greatly harassed and suffering not a little, Saracinesca had one very dangerous shot in his locker. As the little green bird indulged in difficult soprano effects he steered his vessel until he could rake the enemy fore and aft and then his guns belched forth "The Blue and the Gray." The effect was tremendous and there was tumult about. The crowd began to rally around little Italy; and Mr. H. C. Eccles waved his hat and shouted in the purest French: "Beyond the Alps lies Italy," and "The Old Guard dies, but never surrenders."

And the superiority of Yankee Doodle and Dixie over the brass battery's "Cliney" was so manifest that the struggle was all but over, when, in an unfortunate moment, Pietro Ghisleri lost a cog and played a made-in-Germany air that was all beer and skittles, while the Rentfrows, quick to see an advantage, came back with a Cuban love song that had "Mother" in it. This ended the battle. Gambietta retired in good order, but he retired nevertheless. And the little green bird fainted dead away.

Joseph Jefferson

The town will give Mr. Joseph Jefferson a royal welcome when he comes here next month to play "The Rivals." Charlotte knows him only as Rip Van Winkle, and will hardly lose sight of him as Rip Van Winkle no matter how great he may be in "The Rivals." As Rip he wins hearts and a loyalty that he cannot lose. He is many things--an artist, a millionaire, and an actor with versatile talent, yet the world remembers him first and last and best as the droll man who was fond of children and injected humor into sadness. One may not forget the consummate art of Joseph Jefferson. There is none other like him--not one. He is the one to make the clutch come to the throat of a strong man. How curiously he blends humor and sadness--and without effort. The character of Rip Van Winkle cannot stand the test of analysis. He was too far from seriousness, too prone to deceit. As his wife loved him and wept over him and forgave him, he tricked her with a leer and shamed her trusting womanhood. Yet sympathy even here is for the man. Why is he so lovable? Until he was a very old, enfeebled man he showed no depth of feeling, no clearly admirable quality save just that love for children. It is the strange genius of Jefferson that appeals. By a gesture or an expression he touches the wellsprings of mirth and tears. He puzzles. One could feel almost like challenging his right to evoke emotion on such slight pretext. Opinions differ; but in the mind of the writer Jefferson is strongest in both humor and pathos just after he had climbed the mountain and found himself surrounded by sturdy Dutch ghosts who carried kegs. Here was pathos infinite. How?--why? There is no answer. That gaunt figure, that expressive face changed to seriousness, that half frightened effort to be courteous and at ease. . . . It is a simple scene, and yet no man who has seen it will ever forget. He laughs deep in the heart of him and yet could almost weep for memory's sake. . . . How does Jefferson do it? It is the truest humor, the kind that is breathed from the heart with a sigh. There is nothing like the humor and pathos of Joseph Jefferson. You have seen a woman, moved to the depths, laugh softly while her eyes were wet. . . . 'Tis something like that.

Richard Mansfield

Mr. Richard Mansfield and an excellent supporting company presented "Julius Cæsar" at the Academy of Music last night, and pleased the largest theatrical audience that has ever been seen in this city.

For more than four hours the play held the close attention of the audience, yet interest never waned and applause was continuous. Though at the end of the performance disparaging remarks were made by a few captious critics, the general sentiment of the audience was unmistakable. The play and the players had won immense favor.

Mr. Mansfield was a stranger here, though a large proportion of Charlotte people had seen him abroad in other and lighter plays, and waited with curiosity the sterner work that is involved in his interpretation of the character of Brutus. Because of the nature of the play Mr. Mansfield won commendation only gradually. In the first act he figures not largely; in the second act he is not at his best; but in the last four acts his impersonation of Brutus was the mainspring of the play, and at times he was superb in the understanding art that must live on genius.

The correctness of his interpretation of the character of Brutus may be questioned, but it was fascinating. Brutus, portrayed by Mr. Mansfield, was curiously quiet and morose in disposition. Before the assassination of Cæsar, Brutus wore a haunted, wretched look, as if he was a victim of remorse or was oppressed with horrible stage fright. He seemed to pose occasionally, space, and most of his strongest utterances were delivered in a tense, low voice. Inwardly he suffered the agonies of the damned. Outwardly, he was the soul of quietude; except in certain moments when the actor, startling one with the rapidity of the change in his demeanor, became a creature of fire and passion.

Mr. Mansfield made the life of Brutus climatical in a mournful key. Brutus, the noblest Roman of them all, was accursed by a deed committed through a sense of duty; he never tasted happiness; and his mournfulness gave to his life a certain majestic simplicity and resignation that were not lost even in the memorable quarrel with Cassius, or in the ardor of battle. While other men--other conspirators--talked and planned, Brutus stood near by, alone, silent if he might be; brooding with a far-away look on his face.

Mr. Mansfield's conception showed a Brutus who was to be admired or pitied, but not liked; and therefore Mr. Mansfield's success in the character is due to art and art alone. Without effort, or by no high-sounding words, he made himself the central figure on the stage. He seemed to pose occasionally, for, unavoidably, there was posing in the life of Brutus; but it was the simple realism of Mr. Mansfield's part that made it frequently great, and interesting at all times. As an orator or in other incidents of the forum scene, or as a warrior, he was less attractive than in showing bare human touches: the brief scene with Portia; the weariness and suffering in his tent; the love for Cassius and Portia expressed in a look or a gesture; or the terror in the ghost scene-- Mr. Mansfield's personality was there. One marked it in that unforgettably clean and crisp enunciation, in the glare of his odd eyes and in the characteristic tilting of his chin; but if one did not forget Mansfield he yet saw Brutus as a vital being whose honor was supreme and whose suffering was so keen that he looked gladly on death.

Mr. Mansfield's support was well-nigh perfect--in keeping with his reputation for always having a well-balanced company. Mr. Arthur Forrest, in the always popular part of Marc Antony, looked and acted his part in a manner that never failed to provoke prolonged applause. He is a big fellow with an expressive countenance and a voice that he handles remarkably well; and the adroit use of this same voice in the burial scene was very clever indeed. Rivalling Mr. Forrest for honors was Mr. Paulding as Cassius, a part that he sustained wonderfully well. Between these two men and Mr. Mansfield or other leading members of the company there was none of the difference in ability that so often mars a production. The entire supporting company did work that was in keeping with the pace set by Mr. Mansfield. Mr. Arthur Greenaway was a very tired and listless Cæsar, but his resemblance to the supposed visage of the distinguished Roman would have caused one to overlook faults that were not at all serious.

Only two women took leading parts: Miss Maude Hoffman as Calphurnia and Miss Dorothy Hammond as Portia--two characters that were cleverly and gracefully portrayed.

The scenery was magnificent--a typical Mansfield production. No more than that need be said in praise. All the accessories or furnishings of the stage showed the highest point of artistic discrimination; and it may be added that the local Roman recruits who enlisted here did their parts well and added proper color to the stirring mob scenes in the play.

As has been indicated, the play was received with every evidence of great liking. Numerous times Mr. Mansfield was interrupted in his utterances by applause that was general and spontaneous. He resisted even the most prolonged efforts to make him respond to a curtain call. Mr. Forrest, who was a universal favorite, was the only actor who consented to come before the curtain and make his bow.

A Chinese Prima-Donna

The most remarkable grand opera voice that the writer ever heard was in the head of a heathen. 'Twas in Shanghai, and a young swell among the Chinese said he knew about a famous sing-song girl from Soochow who was appearing in one of the native theatres and attracting no end of attention. He invited the writer to go around and hear the vocalizing. The prima donna appeared in a place that was packed with Chinese, who showed as much appreciation as can be given by a stolid and unemotional people. Her small form was clothed in the richest silks; her hair reeked with cocoanut oil and glistened with green jade things and diamonds; her lips were painted to a brilliant red and her feet were compressed to the size of an infant's. In her hand she held a one-string guitar-sort of an arrangement, and as she sang she played an accompaniment. And it is a truth that from the time that little female opened her mouth to sing until she was too exhausted to chirp she held the same weird, high note that provokes fulsome praise from a metropolitan audience. But the high note was all she had in her repertoire; she took it from the jump and couldn't have come under it if she had tried. In other words, she, a heathen--just like lots of heathen--found naturally a thing that civilization in its highest art seeks for incessantly and seldom obtains.

Music at Twilight

And, by the sacred name of St. Cecilia, the thing doesn't seem right. Science, modern improvements and American ingenuity play false economics with art. The woman and the piano are the acme of music, and all the claptrap arrangements can't cheapen the ideal. Even the man who must resist an impulse to join the children who dance to the sound of the street organ will admit that the excessive amount of music-by-machinery has a tendency to keep the woman away from the piano oftener than in former days, yet he and the world that loves music would not have it so. The old-fashioned way is the best. Grand Opera, Duss, Creatore--they have become essentials, but the music that a man reverences comes from the woman and the piano. There is memory of twilight above the half-bowed head; a feminine outline in clean, fresh white; a sure, easy, gentle touch, and then, maybe, a voice, low and full, steals out of the darkened room. This is the musicthat creeps into one's soul and lingers there forever.

A Great Musical Event

The greatest ovation that has ever been tendered to any one in the Academy of Music was given last night to Madame Nordica.

If Madame Nordica had not been in the city, then Monsieur Edouard de Reszke would have been the recipient of this superlative testimonial of liking; and the welcome that was showered upon Mr. John S. Duss and the Metropolitan Opera House orchestra was as spontaneous and almost as warm as the applause that so persistently followed the two great artists.

The concert last night was the chiefest event of artistic character in the life of the community. The playhouse was not so crowded as it has been on one or two occasions, but the great majority of the seats were taken by an audience that represented the culture and intelligence of the best element of North Carolinians. In the assembly were visitors from all parts of the State, and the ensemble as it was seen from the stage was such as to cause both Madame Nordica and Monsieur de Reszke to express delight at their reception here and to say that they had never found readier appreciation in any audience in any part of the world. "I responded to two encores," declared Madame Nordica, who usually does not respond to more than one call from an audience, "because I wished to do so. I liked the atmosphere of sympathy that was created by these people."

For half an hour before the large audience had fully gathered the seventy-five performers of Duss--a well-groomed, fine-looking body of men--sat on a stage, unconcealed by curtain, and exchanged glances with the spectators.

At 8:30 o'clock the opening of the concert was announced by the appearance of John S. Duss--this Duss, who has made fame and fortune and has so consistently pleased discriminating New Yorkers and all other peoples whom he confronts. Beyond being the embodiment of grace and ease there is nothing particularly remarkable in his appearance. Yet you find yourself lazily liking the thoroughness of his bow before he mounts his little stand, and after that--

Well, this man does seem to be in a class by himself. He poses as no freak, like the agile, acrobatic Creatore or others of the Eye-talian school. He appears simply as a gentleman in dress clothes, and he impresses one as being a man who had gone through all the musical schools, had learned all there is to know about music, and yet, retaining all his saneness, is perfectly delighted to appear in simplicity and exercise his knowledge and good taste in bringing unlimited pleasure to everybody.

Mr. Duss conducts that orchestra--conducts it with his body and soul; and it breathes true and fine and strong in response to his slightest gesture. Every number that was given solely by the orchestra was encored and encored, and Duss bowed and bowed and was complacent until further generosity was out of the question. An attempt at analytical criticism of Duss's music would be absurd. The pieces were there--exquisite. And in the hands of Duss they were simpler and better than in the hands of any other man in America.

Then Madame Nordica came! Of course she was superbly dressed. That was an incident. One saw it at a glance and forgot it. This personality was so vital, so likable. She came not wearing stage habit, but as a queenly lady, or, better, a gracious woman. And the house seemed to speak to her as with one voice, and gave her a greeting that has been given to no other stranger that has ever come to this town.

First she sang not the number on the programme, but an aria from Il Trovatore. Here the pencil pauses, and this poor, lame critic would let his hand be palsied before he would endeavor to define the art of Madame Nordica with cold, technical words. Technique! What is that? This woman just sang--sang living, pulsing song, and one fresh from her presence swears that she sang as no one else can sing. She was as simple as a child and as grand as a princess; and her music stole surely into the senses and lingered and helped. God has been very good to this lady.

They showered her with flowers--very many flowers. Among the gifts was a small and beautiful plant that bore one hundred and fifty pure white roses. And again and again the audience begged to be indulged and was gratified. There were never more delighted listeners, never a woman who seemed to be so glad to please.

Such cordial relationship was the keynote of the evening. 'Twas there when Monsieur de Reszke appeared. He was almost swept off his feet by the applause that was only faint testimonial of the great admiration for his big, wondrous voice. He, too, was kindly and acquiescent to every demand; and the ovation reached intensity when at length the two artists appeared and sang together. The evening was one that will live in memory. Nordica--de Reszke--Duss! Ah, the South is being blessed just now!

The local public will be gratified to learn that the concert was a financial success. It would have been exceedingly profitable had it not been for the fact that an exciting political election which was interesting to the greater part of the town unavoidably prevented many persons from going to the Academy.

Nordica

One wonders how Nordica will be judged by the Lord. He gave her that marvellous voice, but through the long years she has worked hard and treasured her talent so that she might give pleasure to thousands upon ten thousands of people. She has done vast and lasting good. Her music has the beautifullest influence. It betters and purifies, somehow. No man with good in him can hear that voice without being refined and eased. Month after month for a quarter of a century and more that voice has been lifting care from tired hearts and brightening lives. The best music is like unto the sweetness of Christianity; and Nordica has had so much of the best to give. At the highest ebb man can do no more than please and bless humanity, and Nordica has done both. Her private life? "It is all right, but suppose it were--anything. The offering of that woman at the last might lift into Paradise a soul as black as Egypt's night.

CHAPTER XIV
REFLECTIONS ON LIFE AND DEATH

Human Wants

The real secret of the greatest happiness consists in the entertainment and gratification of genuine wants, and a curse of living is in the fact that as one grows older his wants decrease in simplicity or ask the impossible. To so live that one may become very hungry and then eat; to become heated and exhausted after a long walk and then to come to a cool spring, surmounted by maidenhair ferns--that is a primitive life that man needlessly parts company with. And the power to want something intensely, in mental or emotional way, is a sign of the fuller living that is marked in few people. To be seized with a fierce desire to do a great thing, or to want a woman until the heart aches--how much of a namby-pamby world understands? . . . It is this power of want that provides the pleasures and sorrows and tragedies, and the heart that want leaves is desolate and dead.

Cattish Thrusts

Do you know that the little mean things you say about people do not die? The way this truth is evidenced here would be amusing if it were not so sad. The firm, outspoken expression of opinion is always tolerable, even if it hurt in condemnation. It is the sly, cattish thrusts that are not forgiven. They may not be big enough for resentment, but they rankle and breed bitterness. Everybody knows everybody else--knows weakness, at least. Be sure of that. The knowledge that we have of one another is one of the ghastliest things in all living. Every man assumes the greatest risk when he sits in judgment upon another man. He is safe and respected only when he does this bravely, with an effort to be fair. You, be you man or woman, who make a practice of doling out malice in confidential utterances--you are marked. This is one of the everyday things that everybody knows to be true. Above all men, the foolish whisper of evil is most despised.

The Tiger in Man

And some one else has said that the greatest trouble about sinning is the mad, useless longing to sin all over again. This is only discursive quotation. The pleasure and peace that are not based on self-denial are not worth a picayune; and there is no positive basis of happiness apart from the Christian religion. For this and for that a man would like to tilt his chin and stroll hellwards, but there is unrest on the way and the sweetness turns bitter as gall. The unhappiness of doing as you please and the happiness of doing as you don't please are as bothersome to Ben, the orphan boy, who drives the donkey, as they are to the fine lady in the frou-frou clothes, and the venerable gentleman who leans on his cane and looks back on seventy years of toil and fretfulness.

The observant man was talking about these things the other day, and he said it was unfair to lay down rules for general application because some people had tigers and some hadn't tigers. By tigers he meant hot, impulsive blood--the ardent temperament that is as apt to curse as to bless; an inherited thing that puts up a fight during a lifetime. The untigered folk are the untempted, serene and patronizing minority who make laws for the rest of mankind. They would accept Utopia as a deserved property, and their certainty of a crown in the hereafter is based upon their lack of wish to do the deeds that send people to the lower regions. They have unlimited satisfaction, but no capacity for suffering, and no fun. The observant man said it was the tigered people who put their arms around you when you wept, and that the other kind didn't understand-- somehow. He said that the chiefest joy in living is to conquer the tiger, but that he'd rather be conquered by it than to never feel the hard, quick leap of the inner breast.

Sympathetic Insight

As a rule, the real students of human nature are the men who say little and make no pretensions to sociological knowledge. As you wander in the crowd you find, now and then, but not often, a man who looks at you with clear, seeing eyes, and you feel that he knows you. He has the faculty of sizing up a man at a glance; which means that he has inherited a great gift, and has made good use of it. He is apt to be the right sort of a man; for any one who understands himself and other men must have sympathy and charity in his heart. He is apt to be a self-contained man who speaks deliberately and kindly, and would prefer to listen to the talk of other people. He knows that weakness in the world is much more prevalent than strength, and that it is very hard indeed for any one to be strong; and so he condones weakness as far as possible and admires strength wherever he finds it. This is a feeble effort to classify the exceptional man who learns to know his fellows through the process of sympathy--and that is the only right way to know mankind. Facing such a man the weakest person is not terrified, for he knows that the bad is not allowed to shroud whatever good there may be, and that the inevitable judgment will not be little, or nagging, or unreasonable. No, you don't fear the man who knows you, but you do fear, and suffer most from, the supercilious person who thinks he knows you, and finds motives where you haven't motives--the person who seeks for evil and broods over your unguarded moments. This man--he moves in legions--is so blinded by conceit that he does not know himself. He is none other than the captious critic who is to be met on every street corner. His infrequent charity lacks tact, and is not helpful because it is not sincere. The other kind of a man, who looks deep into human nature, breaks his silence to speak the charity that keeps the world straight and makes life good and sweet. For the knowing of human nature exacts charity and kindliness, not as virtues, but necessary things.

Flaws

And--make no mistake about this--all your bad qualities are thoroughly known. In this regard no one can fool an individual or a community. Your amiable disposition and your good motives may be misjudged, but the child that stays at your elbow for three days spots the meanness in you. This is a truth that some people seem to learn very late in life, for they are forever leaving down hurtful gaps by picking flaws in the rest of the human herd. When you were very small you may have quarrelled with a brother or a sister, with whom you had been on good terms for a long time. Do you remember how quickly your new enemy turned on you with taunts and showed you that you had been watched narrowly all the while, that every little dirty deed was remembered, every weakness was correctly marked, and that sins and weaknesses, thought to be hidden, were naked under observant eyes? All your life you do not escape from that sort of a game. You can rend and tear and analyze. That is your privilege. But do not be such a fool as to think you deceive anybody about the wrong that is in you; for the notorious knowledge of your faults is a penalty you have to pay for living. This is another one of the little just-so things that people don't stop to think about often enough.

New Year's Resolutions

The world's mind, as a composite proposition, seems to be a feeble, narrow thing at times. Just now all humor seems to hinge on the man who makes New Year's resolutions and breaks them. Puck and Judge, always reeking with common ideas and commoner wit, will be surcharged with such humor at this season; and the other comic papers are printing the same old inane anecdotes. The hackneyed spluttering of humor is heard here; and yet where is the room for laughter? The world swears off and tries to do better. It drops back to old habits. That is tragedy. But it ought to be seriously and solemnly patted on the back for the little spurt. It is something for some men to be decent to their wives for three days; to get sober even for forty-eight hours; an annual miracle when some men taste unselfishness for an hour; and there is wholesomeness even in a faint wish to do better. How foolish and young and ineffectual mankind must look in the eyes of Heaven? Most men want to be good, and can't be good. The world is full of hope--full, too, of brooding sadness that may become intensified by disappointment. There's so much pathos in the weak little wishes. And good, too. The most brutal thing that was ever written was "The road to hell is paved with good intentions." By a token of mercy, a man who honestly has good intentions all the way round has no business being in hell.

The Big Passions

When the big passions work you never know what man is going to do to his fellow man. The story of those women being torn and trampled in the Chicago fire is really an old story in a way. The normal man cannot conceive that he will ever be worked up to the point where, through fright, he would crush or slay a woman or a child, yet to such pitch of frenzy seeming good men are sometimes roused. The thought of what a man may do because of fear and may or may not do because of love suggests alarming possibilities. In ordinary situations a man is schooled and can depend upon himself. He is an educated creature who has imbibed creeds and rules that spell civilization. But underneath it all there is the primeval man, the animal thing that is reasonless, fierce, and may be cruel beyond expression when, by some untoward chance, it is provoked into quick, ruthless action. It is ghastly to see anything that is thoroughly frightened. Fear on the face of a beast is both pitiful and revolting, but in all living there is scarcely anything that is so appalling as a man who is convulsed by fear; and the worst fear is that which faces a man unexpectedly, gives him no time for preparation, scatters his other senses, and puts the look of an animal behind human eyes. Such fear has no real likeness to cowardice. It strikes while cowardice whimpers and covers its eyes. Neither quality is forgivable, though, like the character of a fool, it is no more than a badge of ancestry.

The fearful man is most to be feared. Once the writer saw a man run amuck. He was a great, powerful East Indian. Heat or drink worked on his brain, and he ran out of a dive in an eastern port, irresponsible, with treble strength, and with an unthinking lust to slay. Even as he charged a crowd, with the wild intent of murder, it was seen that no bravery was on his face. 'Twas fear. The great awakened spirit of fear was in his rolling eyes and governed his powerful limbs. Fear of himself! Some devil of fear was leaping in him. It hurled him to the supremest ebb of emotion--was the greatest sensation he could feel. Such things are not good to look upon and let live, and so they jammed back into a corner and slew him, though even as he fought back with the energy of a maddened tiger his face pictured the fear that tore at his vitals and came out to stamp horror on a face that was dead.

There is another kind of fear that is also unforgivable. Years ago the writer read an odd little story and somehow he has never forgotten it. A man and a woman were out driving. They were engaged. Both were all they should have been. So much was told by suggestion. The horses, big black fellows, ran away. Faster and faster they went, and death or great bodily harm seemed inevitable. The man thought only of the woman. He thought rapidly, sensitively. He saw in imagination a crash, saw the woman dragged under the wheels of the vehicle and mutilated. . . . He would have leaned over and seized her with violent, tender strength and lifted her out of danger. As the spasm of fear struck him he leaped from the buggy. A second later he would have surrendered his soul if he could have undone his act. His fear for the woman had governed him. Yet he had jumped. A little further on there was a collision, and the woman was thrown out and only slightly injured. She arose and faced the man. There was nothing to say, or rather everything was said in a look. She, by some intuition, understood him perfectly; did not misjudge his motive. He knew she understood. But he had jumped. 'Twas wearisome--that knowledge, but neither could ever forget. That was the end. The story is fruitful with ideas. So many people jump; or lose happiness or reputation by the action of a second. When the big sleeping things awake, what then? . . . God knows.

Reflections in a Churchyard

While loitering in an old churchyard in Cheraw, S. C., a few days ago, Mr. J. F. Ware, of this city, found a tomb that is evidently very old, though it bears no date. On the broad marble slab at the top is this inscription:

> "My name--my country--what are they to thee?
> What--whether high or low my pedigree?
> Perhaps I far surpassed all other men.
> Perhaps I fell below them all--what then?
> Suffice it, stranger, that thou seest a tomb.
> Thou know'st its use; it hides no matter whom."

One would like to have known the man who wrote the verse. There is in the words the easy, sarcastic challenge of a man who has lived life his own way and is satisfied to go down at the end in gaunt solitude, leaving only a taunt for the world behind that would have disturbed his privacy in looking for a lying epitaph. Maybe he had both found and lost happiness. Maybe he had tasted pleasure to its depths; maybe he had sinned and blundered and suffered and had dabbled in all the little human things that eat away the joy of life. So! Let it pass at that. He would be shielded in his shroud; obliterated; forgotten eternally. Strange yet understandable pride! Tombstones--some tombstones--grow hoary with age in spelling a hideous lie--screaming virtues above dry bones that cannot escape the mockery. This man wanted his tomb to say nothing except to rebuke curiosity. Here lies a dead man! He has played out the game--how or when it is none of your affair. There was a brief tilt with Fate, and when Death came he saw only one last inscrutable smile and a slight shrug of the shoulders. The man-thing, blown to life from feeble clay, had played his part, not servilely or in fear of the little frowning gods created here below, and he would go back to dust and stay as dust under the canopy where human breath flutters but little longer than the daisies grow.

The question has been asked, Would you, if you were allowed to do so, live your life all over again? The query calls forth profitless thought, but would you? Would you be willing or glad to start at the beginning and go through--everything again? Think! Look back, count pleasure and grief, peace and unrest. Does it, as a whole, seem good and sweet to you? Would you consent to take up the sorrow for the sake of the happiness that came to you? If you say yes, then you may be one of two kinds of people--a fine healthy animal who loves the memory of basking in the sunshine, or a person whose senses were strung taut in the keenness of living and yet, seeing both the lights and the shadows, is not afraid or ashamed. There is a third element which need not be considered. In this there be those who look back hopelessly . . . here a restless majority who cling to the future as the only salvation in a maelstrom--as against loss irretrievable. 'Tis a pleasant pastime to speculate about the quality of hell that awaits the other man--and easier, rather, than to gaze into the nice, yawning little hell that we may have builded right here on our own account. Probably you'd better not start to thinking on this subject.

A Bartender's View

"Whiskey drinking," said the old barkeeper, "is the curse of the world, but men will drink so long as men are men. Since I have been passing drinks across the counter I have seen all manner of tragedies, and it is a mistake to suppose that a bartender grows callous, though his life would be easier if he were like that. We must be polite and attentive, but I have seen the time when it was hard to keep from being a mere man and preaching temperance as I handed liquor to a customer. Our life affords unlimited study of human nature. I have seen all the gradations, and after years of thought I have reached a few conclusions that are not new. One man in a thousand may drink safely. The others are threatened always, and this side the danger-line they are travelling with a curb bit. The man who sticks to three drinks a day is a miracle. A man who inherits a thirst from his father and grandfather may be a teetotaller until he is fifty, but he may expect delirium tremens any time after he ceases to be a total abstainer. I have seen a town bum sober up and become a respectable member of society, and I have a good deal of faith in the Keeley cure; but the gentleman who begins to get drunk after he is thirty years old might as well shoot himself and save his family physician the necessity of lying as to the cause of his death. I have never known but one man who had the jim-jams to escape a drunkard's death. Paralysis saved him. Whiskey is mankind's strongest common love. It is the best medicine in the world, and as a means of killing off surplus population it is surer, though slower, than the Black Death."

The King Drug

The new sanitarium around the corner advertises that it will cure the drug habit and drinking by the immediate withdrawal policy, and says that the patient will suffer no evil effects or inconvenience therefrom. He will be made a normal man who normally doesn't care for stimulants or narcotics. That sounds pretty, and this is to be no criticism of the new method; but it is permissible for one to imagine that the gentleman who has been having pipe dreams for a quarter of a century will not be singing psalms of jubilation during the first few days after the morphine has been removed. More than all the gods in the world, the king drug receives faithful homage, and his gaunt hands forever tug at the vitals of the devotees who would be deserters from his shrine. Quit morphine! Have you ever seen any one quitting morphine? Quit the king drug and smile; writhe on the rack and laugh--'tis the same. Whiskey means unrest and worry. Morphine gives the only artificial sensation that is flawless. A morphine existence looks upon realism as a horrid purgatory--as a rude awakening from a fanciful, soothing heaven. 'Tis so. Quitting comes after the sweat of agony beads the forehead and the teeth are jammed hard against the lip. Morphine is the thing that the Lord makes people pay dearest for playing with. It brings too much happiness not to demand misery. If the latter end of morphine and the quitting of morphine did not mean a circumscribed but sure hell, every other person that one met on the streets would have dreamy, unseeing eyes. Oh, the philosophy of the doctor people is all right: the only way to do a thing is to do it. But no man who falls under the spell of the king drug or whiskey ever quits either without the ineffable torture of White Nights--the hard, dry clutch at the throat, the ache of punished nerves, and the grim, wearisome struggle over sickened manhood.

And the lesser evil, thirst--do you know what that is? Perhaps you have toiled along in the sunshine without water and then you have thought of a trickling spring under moss-covered rocks. Perhaps you have been so fever-stricken that you thought only of the parching and the easement. You call this thirst, and yet it is as a child's careless wish compared to that other thing--the devilish thirst that plays with a man and shakes him like a reed in the wind. . . . Restlessness, the gripe and the gnaw, the tongue that will not moisten, the hands that sink nails into flesh, the voice that must be stifled from screaming, the vain cry against thralldom, and then once more the fierce, keen, surging want that shivers the very soul in its madness and intensity. So! That is thirst.

Blind!

"I am going down to the hospital to tell a young man that he will never see again," said an eye specialist a few days ago. "He will be surprised. His eyes have been affected only a few days." Afterward the specialist performed an operation that permitted the young man to see just enough out of one eye to keep out of the way of other people. He will never read again; never again see appreciatively the beauties of the universe. The incident will be marked as ordinary, though sad, and yet it is a tragedy worse than death. Death is kinder than a living hurt that does not die, and blindness is a part of the loss-wail which cries the grief universal. Blindness as a physical evil, weakness to replace strength, or the loss of character, or the end of love--these sum up bitterer distress than grief before a bier. To have a thing and lose it. Here is the large spring of tears--here mankind's kinship in feebleness. Lost! 'Tis the most direful word in the language. It is God's term to describe a condition that we know not of, and it is given to man to wear it as a badge of worst mourning. The telling of all sorrow that one knows could begin with that one word. To live after remembering happiness that is dead; to breathe and be mocked by the ghost of sweetness; to lose beyond recall--so comes the tragedy and the pathos. Lost! Blind! There are so much of both. Loss this side the grave is the worst, after all; and the most grewsome death's head is on real flesh and blood.

Such unpleasant reflection came involuntarily. One shudders in the face of the calamity that befell the young man, and his condition appeals for sympathy. He will probably live for a long time, and one thinks of the great test that is placed upon his bravery, for he must now totter as a memorial to loss. Every minute all his fortitude will be required. The story will remind Charlotte people of John Schenck, who was the most active and one of the happiest and most successful young men in this city. Suddenly he went blind. The thing seemed inconceivable. His life had been so promising; he had gloried in what he saw; he had so much to do. But, stricken, he crept to his home and died through the space of three years; and one thinks now that maybe heaven blessed him that way. For he beautified and enriched the little life that was left to him; made it a plea for unselfishness and a story of love; triumphed over affliction; and his passing was in sweetness and without fear. Viewing the test that was placed upon John Schenck and others who are openly struck with a heavy hand, there is wonder as to the credit that will be allowed for living just an ordinary life in which no very severe demand is made on endurance. As a man grows older he ceases to rail at the cause of suffering; for through suffering comes purification and the best in life. Usually the best people are the happiest, but the best happiness is the kind that comes after or through unhappiness. This shines and blesses with its radiance.

Death

As the years pass you find there is such a lot of death, and you have not lived long before you realize that most of life is dying. No one that you know is spared the touch of the moulded fingers. And as you are forced to look upon the Thing it becomes less terrible and in a stupid, useless sort of way you can reason about it. You find that after all it is a pretty easy sort of a matter to die and that there are comparatively few people who have not died. You learn that the little books that tell about the horrors of death-bed scenes show a picture that is not usually seen, for in the great majority of cases you see that the mental dread of death decreases as the body becomes weaker, and the passing is quiet and without complaint or fright. As you live and see you discover what has always been known--that the most natural event in all life is dying, and the gaunt, grim Spectre terrorizes only where he grapples unawares and arranges to blot out to-day the mind that had every reason to expect to be vigorous on the morrow. The sudden death that in an instant transforms flesh and brain to clay may be kind, but the ghastliest sound in nature is the surprised whimper of a man who turns from revelling in the sunshine to find himself dangling over the last abyss--fresh with the fulness of living, yet full of the knowledge that death cannot be denied. This is, or may be, hell.

This is the kind of death that shudders all mankind and screams a tale of incompleteness and the neglect of sacred duties. At the Southern depot two years ago a young man stepped off a train and was struck by a switch engine, the lower part of his body being crushed to bits. He was carried into the baggage room and laid high on a box; a physician examined him and shook his head, and the crowd stepped back and waited. Here were all the elements of a tragedy. The man didn't suffer; he was intensely alive, acutely conscious, and he knew he couldn't live two hours. His voice, desperately strong, told his misery in a dozen sentences. And it was an old story. He had just trifled with things. There was a mother, and she was a devoted mother; and some day he had expected to settle down and be worthy of her goodness, but--the brow was now damp with death sweat. There was another woman. . . . He pulled a package of letters from his pocket, fumbled them and tried to read-- and then spoke on. This woman--she had been gentle and faithful and young and tender, and he had intended, some time, to quit being unworthy, and show her that he could love unselfishly. But now! There was nothing that was worth while to say, but he talked as if he could never have done with speaking. He spoke, not incoherently, but feverishly, as against time; and one knew that he wanted to get up and scream a protest that it was all a mistake, that the summons had come too quick, that he had so many things to do--so very many things to say and do. His brain was keen in its understanding. He saw his whole life in an instant; saw the profitless years; recognized all his latent power for good, and now knew that the good in him was being stifled for an eternity. And as he would have continued to speak in weird, fearful fretfulness, Death struck contemptuously and the wail went elsewhere.

An Unfulfilled Dream

What becomes of the great human good that is killed before it has a chance to exercise an influence? This is a question that arises out of the thought of another local tragedy. There was a woman here who was all that she should have been. Through ten years or more she loved a man and was engaged to him. She did well all her duties, but her whole mind and heart became centred on her marriage. She waited patiently enough, and the thought of her wedding day kept her heart young, though the touch of white came to her hair. Then, at last, the time came. Her house wore green and white; there were carriages in front of the door and an unmistakable bustle inside. For years the bride had read accounts of other people's weddings, and she wanted a reporter at her wedding. He went and was taken into a bedroom where a woman lay nigh unto death. But her face was enraptured. Every other person in the room looked anxious, but the bride was in ecstacies. This was her wedding day--a day that all her living had been shaped to meet. And, so, she was married. Because she was just a woman and a bride the reporter was a man to be considered, and she spoke to him with a girlish flush on her face and a quiver in her voice. Would he make them show him the decorations and her wedding clothes? They were pretty clothes, she thought, and all of them she had made herself--had made years and years ago. Would the reporter please. . . . And the reporter did--did write all that a man may be allowed to write, and then, three days later, wrote an account of the death of the bride. But what became of all her preparation, of all her big, beautiful thoughts, of her deep, simple wish to be a good wife and, please God, a good mother.

"Just Tired"

"The saddest and strangest incident I ever saw was a suicide in Kansas City a few years ago," said a traveling man at the Buford. "A revolver shot was heard in one of the rooms of the hotel and those of us who hurriedly entered the room found a young man lying dead. He had shot himself through the heart and had died almost instantly. He was a singularly handsome fellow, well groomed and carefully dressed. I remember noticing the fineness of his linen, the slender links in his watch chain, the graceful fit of his clothes, and his strong, well-kept hands. And his face suggested strength and character without trace of weakness. Some man in the room groaned: 'My

God! The boy has made a mistake. He had no business to die.' On the table next to the bed was the pencilled explanation.

" 'Just tired.'

"There was also on the table a sealed letter to a woman. That was all. The young man was well-known and the papers had a lot to say about his suicide, but no cause was ever assigned. After everything was said the world merely knew that for reason sufficient unto himself the man had wanted to die and had died. There was no suggestion of his insanity. He was tired and his life went out at that."

In the Western world men say in kindness, kind or unkind, that a self-murderer suffered from temporary aberration of the mind, and the words are supposed to bring surcease of sorrow to relatives. The saying is natural in a way, for to the ordinary, healthy mind the thought of suicide, of deliberately sending one's self into eternity, is ghastly and revolting. To look with clear eyes upon sunlight, to hear the laughter of children, to see the beauty in all nature--and then to take the privilege of deity and send out a blackened, restless soul into the unknown! . . . The mind grasps such things feebly, and, in knowing suffering, shudders at the limitless possibilities of human agony. Insanity? So! It is better so to think. Moreover, self-death is termed rank cowardice, which, in evident contradiction, seeks eternal chastening. To punish a palpitating thing that suffered till it wanted to die! 'Tis hard to conceive of that.

Murder

I tell you there is something ghastly in the thought of killing a Thing that can think and talk and love and yet has such a little while in which to shape the destiny of an immortal soul. For a mere man to take the prerogatives of deity and fix the time when that Thing shall float out into the Unknown--ah, that is awful! What room for brooding! "I am eternally prodding myself by puzzling over what the other fellow might have done if he had been allowed to live," was the remark made to me by a man who had happened to fire first.

"Justification--justified!" Oh, the cynical jest! The judge and jury fade away, but it is a poor, triumphant figure who stalks away into White Nights--into the black land of Remorse. He lies when he says he finds easement. He is so branded and seared within himself that his brain, stung beyond hope of cure, will agonize him till he dies.

A man's wrestle over his own soul is the most stupendous tragedy. What added and terrible burden there must be in being forever shrouded with the grave clothes of another man--in conjuring visions of staring eyes and dank hair and in speculating about the soul that rudely found unripe freedom. Such poor leavings are these when full passion has been gratified.

The Death-cap

In the numerous cases of murder that have been recently reported in the papers, you have perhaps noticed that the murderers, or those who have been charged with murder, have invariably been characterized as showing a cool, bold front. Sometimes they have been jocular, and Mr. H. E. C. Bryant says that James Wilcox, who was charged with the murder of Nellie Cropsey, actually looked happy. Molineux was never for a moment disconcerted or abashed; and coming to the small fry of the defendants--to those who are admittedly guilty, you find uniform self-possession, if not bravado. All over the country there are men who are facing, or standing on, the gallows with a laugh on their lips; and the single cry of repentance and plea for mercy come from the wretch who is suddenly made to face the burning fagots. Murderers--all murderers, seemingly--face trial easily and death easily; and there are only a few cases to show the retribution that is supposed to operate this side of the grave. The law, in the fine, savage limit of its vengeance, seems impotent, and is mocked by the last jeering words that are mumbled in the death-cap. A snake has bitten and a snake has crushed, but it dies--a snake.

All history shows the operation of this defiant spirit, and one is forced to come to the conclusion that the real punishment for the deliberate murderer begins only beyond the gallows. You kill him, and that is an easy matter and a precaution against further crime, but all the sternness and justness of justice fail to bow a stubborn head or bring remorse to a gloating heart. This places a murderer in a distinctive class. You can't get at him and you can't know him any more than you can know the workings of the heart of a tiger. He has wanted very much to do a thing and he has done it, and he stays on the high tide of his exultation till he faces That which made him and can make him suffer.

This is a cursory study of bad men who have had time, through the processes of the law, to prepare for death. A man can be keyed up to do anything. You are, so far as you know, perfectly well, but if within the hour a physician were to tell you that you had a mortal disease, your mind, horrified at first, would in a very short time begin to adjust itself to the new condition and would prepare you to face the end with equanimity. But if you, without warning and while in the flush of best strength, found death at your elbow, you, being an ordinary sort of a man, would suffer terror indescribable. The murderer is given the physic--wait, or time for preparation. Without that--if his punishment were immediate--he would probably meet the end as a trembling coward.

A Crude Tragedy

Almost every day one hears of a man killing a woman for apparently trivial cause. The normal man wonders. There is possible extenuation when one man strives equally with a fellow man and slays him to save his own life. But the thing in a human being that will cause him to murder the female of his kind is not to be analyzed, though it is uppermost in the annals of crime.

Within the last three years in this city three colored men have slain women, two of the criminals being wife-murderers. In all three cases, so far as the public could see, the excuse or provocation for murder was the nagging spirit of the women. In one instance a woman followed a man and taunted and worried him. In another a wife flaunted disobedience in the face of her lord and master; and in the last case--when Pauline Gabriel was killed last week--the wife nagged her husband when he was hungry.

Lee Gabriel had been working hard and he came home very hungry. Moreover, he had brought home some white beans. And his wife wouldn't cook his dinner and nagged him. His mind, dwelling upon the tragedy, drones out these things, making the razor and the axe and the horrible blows all incidental features. He was very hungry. There were the beans. She wouldn't cook. He slew her. And he sobs and swears he loved her and adds, in simplicity, that the beans were good beans.

Gabriel was not a degenerate. He was just crude, primeval. Every day his white brothers put to death women and leave the task of assigning cause to the rest of mankind. Oftentimes the murderers merely remember that there were words and words, and the brute stifled life in his weaker kind. One thing only is always clearly visible, and this is the power of a woman's tongue to infuriate a man to the point of madness. Merely on this point the world agrees. A bad woman is the worst thing that is allowed to live; and a nagging woman has a nice tendency to direct people hellwards.

The Image of Death

"What form of death do you prefer?" questioned the observant resident. "Standing on your feet--with your boots on? Well, that's the way most men wish to die. They want it to come right quick. But about the form of death--do you think of death as coming in any particular way? Yes. Well, most people do. You will find that nearly every man who reflects much on the subject always associates dying with a certain scene or method--sometimes with one disease, and sometimes with a particular locality. Maybe there is in your mind the picture of an old graveyard, where ivy clings above ancient tombstones, and you think of this and death as coming together. I know a man, and when he thinks of death he sees at once an old mill-pond that was near his boyhood's home--a mouldy old pond where snags protruded and where frogs croak dismally at night. Dying to him means being pressed down in a place like that; and most other men have mental pictures that stand as vivid conceptions of death. It is one of the greatest blessings that no person can really imagine himself dead. The only likeness to it is sleep, but sleep is sweet. To the normal person death seems suffocation--first. Beyond that he doesn't let himself think, but shudders. The great comfort is that when Nature handles the affair nobody has any terror. A man's horror of death decreases in proportion as he becomes physically weak; and ghastly death-bed scenes are usually the product of an imagination that wishes to frighten the wicked."

The House of Death

How did the man die? 'Tis a question that the world asks about everybody. In childhood one thinks about death as a far-off day--a day when no one is allowed to whistle in the house and when people enter the front door without knocking and know where to go without being told. There is the gloomy, still church, the faint rustle of women's garments, the becraped heads leaning low, the slow, melancholy music, and the solemn words that bespeak the littleness of man and the reason for his peace. And you wonder.

CHAPTER XV
MISCELLANY

Two Kinds of Courting Men

"I am always noticing two kinds of courting men," remarked a citizen who has long acted as an usher at one of the local churches. "A man comes to the church door and his eyes roam over the place until he finds the woman he is looking for. If he walks up the aisle and sits in front of the woman so she can look at him he is one kind of a courting man. But if he is satisfied to take a back seat so that he can see the woman and cannot be seen he is another kind of a suitor and much the better kind. Oh, these little things show character. And it would be dangerous to marry any man who would rather be looked at by a woman than to look at her."

"Drunks and Downs"

"Only drunks and downs to-night," said the turnkey at the police station. "No cases of any importance whatever: only drunks and downs." Only a rudderless derelict in the maelstrom; only a mind besotted by a curse; only a soul engulfed; only a man chained to the body of death!

Harmlessly Insane

There is a man in this county who was harmlessly insane for several years--just touched in the head in a way that did not interfere with his health or liberty. And he was happy--so happy. The world was rose-hued to him, and he had the most innocent, yet fantastic delusions about himself--his cleverness and what people thought of him. He lived with his dream gods always, and had never a care or sorrow. Then they sent him away and cured him; and now he worries about taxes and his cotton crop, and beats his dog. They pulled him out of Wonderland, and now an extra soda biscuit or mettlesome corns make him curse destiny. They did right, of course. He has forgotten how to smile. Those whom the gods would destroy they sometimes refuse madness.

Dreams and Nightmares

"Dreams! What are dreams!" said Dr. Charles F. Brem. "Some man has said that they are the result of one part of the brain entertaining another part. An odd, quaint idea. I wonder?"

"Nightmares! Did you ever have nightmares?" asked Mr. George W. Campbell. "Nightmares suggest future punishment to me. Some part of a man just leaves him and suffers. I have wondered if the thing that suffers in a nightmare doesn't travel around after death, to be tortured in a cramped sort of way."

'Tis an eerie idea.... to go through the countless centuries shuddering with little moans, a baffled, frightened victim of regret that will not die. To feel forever the gloom and to see not clearly--to realize the utter horror of the worst nightmare, and know no easement--that is a fearful conception. This reminds one, somehow, of Dickens's picture of punishment as portrayed in his story about Scrooge and Marley. There the spirit drifted and wailed uselessly over lost opportunities--saw error and couldn't rectify it; witnessed pain and could offer no balm. Such was the agony of remorse. The wonder-- the vain, puzzled wonder....

But dreams be sweet, too--so sweet that man hugs his best dream to his heart and will not tell it. And day dreams--do you know them? They gather behind the sternest brow, and they show a dear, secret world. What matter if you are a hero or a heroine--what matter if the ugly duckling sees herself crowned a princess--what matter if you hear the plaudits of successful ambition? You may not laugh at the dreamers of the day--these folk who build the best without ever attaining it. To tilt the chin and look out into a land where peace and happiness are--to be simple and fine, and to be judged as that; to witness the unselfishness that really is not! 'Tis not bad. To feel the nearness of understanding, the closeness of sympathy, to be protected by Love, an eternal comrade.... Foolish! Ay. And sweet.

The Gods of the East

Those big old gods, by the way, were about the most interesting things the writer saw in the East. They are fascinating frauds, and they play such an important part in the life about. Now, there was Sheng, the millionaire mandarin in China, who in many respects was as modern as a progressive New Yorker. Sheng promised that if his father got well, he, Sheng, would go to Poo-too, the place of many temples, and do much honor to all the gods. The father did get well. Sheng sailed for Poo-too, and the writer had the good fortune to be on his ship. In this place which contains very ancient gods and temples, priests and no women, Sheng made his devoirs and spent $40,000 in one day. He had in him no more spiritual essence than a cat. He had made a promise, and, to use common parlance, he fulfilled it by delivering the goods to the gods. Those Eastern gods are just practical propositions. They live within a stone's throw of your house, and you can go to them at any time and burn paper money before their thrones--tell them that you are in a plagued bad fix and beseech them in pity's name to hurry up and help you out of a hole.

But in one roadside temple and before one divinity there was a scene that will live forever in memory. This lacked not in spiritual quality. Here was a golden goddess, whose placid face scarcely concealed an expression of indifference or disdain. She received prayers that were more sincere than any that were offered to all other deity. Men passed her by, but before her throne women grovelled in the dust in the abandon of entreaty--childless women, agonized.

An Inland Derelict

In this State the gods laughed at a man and let him go to Congress. He had been a successful young lawyer who lived in a small town. He was happy in a careless, well-fed life, and the study of his profession was a recreation. His social life was all that he cared for it to be. After a few years in Washington he came home with link cuffs, his first dress suit, and hungriness in his eyes. They gave him a party where they had lemonade as a chaser, and he remembered a Washington theatre party and high-balls. He hadn't seen enough of a big life to be a man of the world; and he was always drawing comparisons that made him miserable. The small town bored him stiff, and he got into the fatal habit of not listening to the idle talk of his friends. His sole wish was to get away from the place and go back to Washington, or hold some other political office. He is living now, though he is not especially interested in the fact. He has lost the links to one of his cuffs and his clothes are shiny in spots. He will be evermore praying for political lightning to strike him again. Until it does--and it won't--he is so disordered and misplaced as to deserve characterization as an inland derelict.

The Story of a Picture

The newspaper man noticed that women--many women--stopped in front of the show window of Houston, Dixon & Company yesterday and looked at a picture. And as they looked their faces grew interested and thoughtful, for there is something about the picture that challenges attention. It is a cleverly done thing, by C. Allan Gilbert, and is called "The End of a Love Story." It shows a man and a woman in a darkened room. The woman is in a whitish evening dress, and is lying outstretched on a long lounge. Her opera cloak is thrown slightly from her shoulders, and her hair is a bit dishevelled and falls back wavily. Every line of her body suggests rest, relaxation. At first glance she seems to be asleep, but as one looks closer he sees that she is not asleep, and that her lowered lashes do not hide the strange, steady expression of peace, yet wonderment, that is in her eyes.

Her eyes rest upon the man who kneels at her side. There is no affectation in his pose. His face is turned, and one sees only the back of a well-poised head and the outline of firm, clear-cut features. His head is bowed above broad shoulders, and his lips touch the woman's hand. The room is cosy, comfortable. It is a man's room. Thick curtains are parted at a window that looks out upon a darkening street, and a book, opened, lies face down at the window ledge. One imagines that it is just eventide, and that a cheery fire burns in the grate.

Attached to the picture there is a little placard which explains everything. The woman's people wanted her to marry a rich suitor and had worried her, and so she had left her home and come to the man she loved, putting herself absolutely in his hands.

And the man, with fineness, strength and humility portrayed in every line, had knelt at her side and had dared only to touch her hand with his lips. She looks unabashed, unashamed, secure. The man is grateful beyond words. One knows that. Maybe he finds heart to breathe a prayer. Maybe he struggles to keep down the gulp that rises in his throat. One knows that neither of the two has spoken for some time--that neither will speak for a while. Some things are not said in words.

But why the name--why "The End of a Love Story"? Can there be irony in the title? The woman has a good, strong face, too, but there is utter languidness about her. She is Beauty at ease--yet Beauty in splendor. Her proud finery seems yet out of place in the simple room.

The end of a love story? Did she bring self-abnegation with her? Will she grieve when the opera cloak and the other satinish things are taken away? Is she even now thinking that possibly she has made a mistake? Has she one tinge of regret over what she has done? Is this the cynical ending that is meant?

Oh, no; not that. The end is just the beginning. The woman is a little tired now--and she has a right to be tired, hasn't she? She is young and tender, and she has done a very brave thing. She needs the abandon that is in her pose. Her weariness is womanish, with no lack of womanliness. And she feels the great gentleness and reverence that are in the room . . . feels glad that the world is on the outside; and she will be happy forever and forever.

The end is the beginning, and through all the years to come the man and the woman are to stand side by side and look out peacefully upon the gathering shadows.

And the man is sure of himself and his woman, and so he dares to kneel and touch her in utter thankfulness.

Love Letters in Court

The English have a nice little bold custom that doesn't seem to obtain here. Once the writer was over in Yokohama when the British court was trying a woman for the murder of her husband. She was a clean-built, aristocratic specimen, and her husband was a big-hearted chap who had an impassioned sort of fondness for his horses and his dogs and his clubs and his children and his wife. He must have gotten on her nerves in some way, for she fell to putting arsenic in the things that he ate. She was clever enough, and afterward the physicians admitted this. She was not in a bit of a hurry; but she sat by the side of her husband and dosed him gradually. He was not satisfied to have anybody nurse him but his wife, and so she used to keep the long watches of the night with him; and when he grew feverish or suffered she used to smooth his brow with cool, patrician hands and then give him nourishing drink that contained only a reasonable amount of poison. Because she had thorough charge of the situation and was unsuspected, the wife took her own sweet time and slowly murdered her husband through a period of two weeks. Subsequently, people said he had a look of horrible apprehension in his eyes, and that he clung to his wife in a way that was both pitiable and pathetic.

But the wife had a maid who watched through key-holes and got into a habit of picking up pieces of letters from waste baskets and piecing them together. And the maid told things, and Mrs. Carew--for that was her name--was arrested and tried for her life.

My! What a sensation ensued. Mrs. Carew was a dreamy, æsthetic woman who would know just exactly what you meant if you called her "spirit of old-fashioned roses." A good many men had said things like that to her, and the maid had patched up correspondence to show this. The Austrian consul, who was a diplomat, left for home by the first boat, but a well-known bank man did not leave and was put on the witness stand. Mrs. Carew was the kind of a woman who plaintively told only a few people that she was misunderstood by her husband, and the bank man was one of the few. He was so sympathetic--thought she was too fine a creature to be mated to the big frank fellow who was always talking of riding to the hounds; and he said as much in letters that breathed a monopoly of understanding.

And they made that bank man sit up there on the witness stand before a crowded court room and read his own letters to the woman. By this time everybody knew she had committed a fiendish murder; yet the bank man had to read aloud to His Worship and the jury epistles that almost deified the woman. The written love-making was not overdone, not fulsome, but delicate, exquisite. It would have flushed the face and honored the soul of a good woman who was not already a wife; but what a ghastly, horrid sound the words made as the pallid-faced man uttered them in that dreary court room. "You, heartsease"; "dear, tender woman"; "reverence"; "heartfelt appreciation of your unhappiness and its cause"--these were some of the words that the man had written and was forced to read as a token of his shame. He had not been a criminal, but a colossal dupe, which is worse than being a criminal. Ugh! It was awful!

Now, how would it feel to be taken over yonder in the court house and be placed on the stand within a few feet of Judge Neal and just in front of Solicitor Webb? You are handed a letter and you recognize your own handwriting. You are directed to open the letter and read. You are facing all sorts of people that you know and don't know. You painfully clear your throat and start out with:

"Oh, my blooming, beaucheous angel," or some other little commonplace term that you keep out of your business correspondence. You would be so frustrated over your position that you would probably remind yourself of the young man who was so bothered by the litigation over his father's estate that he declared he was almost sorry the old man had ever died. You would really wish that you never knew what a darling or a dearest was, wouldn't you?

You see, a letter is a terrible thing. Rather than write a letter on an important matter, one of the biggest men in this State will get on the train and ride five hundred miles--just to talk only a few minutes. And a letter to a woman may prevent a man from lying as he ought to lie. If he hasn't written a letter, then he should perjure himself, of course, and he will be cursed if he doesn't commit perjury. It is Capt. Harrison Watts who tells the story that has been referred to previously in this connection. A member of a crack Southern club, while on the witness stand, was asked if he had ever kissed a certain woman. He said "I decline to answer." A few hours later the governing officers of his club met and expelled the man from the club, declaring that the only answer a gentleman could make to such a question must be "No."

"A Groundhog Case"

Never was such fine early spring weather as there was just after Mr. McD. Watkins, of this township, shot the groundhog. 'Twas the only groundhog in Mr. Watkins's neighborhood, and that hog was a disgruntled pessimist if there ever was one. He had his home in a hole on the bank of a creek, and he tried to play as much devilment as possible with the six weeks of weather that were under his exclusive control. 'Twas different when he was quite a young, blithe pig. Then when he made arrangements to come out at his regularly appointed time--on February 2d--he would appear at a darksome or cloudy time of day so that, not being able to see his shadow, he might secure a lengthy period of Italian skies and the early blossom of spring onions. But as the groundhog grew older and older he suffered from dyspepsia or something, and he took a peculiar pleasure in commemorating his day by strolling around in the sunshine and watching his awesome shadow, knowing full well that he was working for the deluge. Mr. Watkins said he simply grew tired of the perversity of that groundhog--which, remember, was the only groundhog in the neighborhood--and at length he determined to act in the premises of the distinguished prophecy.

Came a February 2d in the seventies, and Mr. Watkins concealed himself, with a shot-gun in his hand, and watched the mouth of the groundhog's hole. In the forenoon and until late afternoon the rain rained right heavily, and Mr. Watkins knew that if the elements continued beclouded the groundhog would be helpless even if 'twere a case of root-hog-or-die. But the shower ceased and the sun's rays fell glimmeringly. Suddenly the nose of the groundhog appeared, then his head, then his body and then his tail--until he was all out of the hole. He had an evil smile on his face, for he thought that in a minute he would be gazing upon his shadow and then farewell to fair weather. He walked out, with his shadow following quite closely behind him. And he dallied with his shadow like a cat playing with a mouse. There his shadow was, right in the rear, and all he had to do was to turn around and inspect it. He appeared to tease himself into a state of pleasurable anticipation, and, having exhausted this emotion, his eyes revolved and he slowly began turning his head. But before he could so much as rest his optics upon the tip end of his shadow nose, Mr. Watkins fired and the groundhog died--in the very act of an evil forecast. Of course it couldn't rain after that, and Mr. Watkins was voted a vote of thanks and a prize chromo by his appreciative neighbors.

The Judge

After an experience of a great many years, I have concluded that the worst judge is the harsh man who is judge. He doesn't deceive even himself when he punishes every offender to the utmost degree and then declares that he merely enforces the law. I never saw a harsh judge who didn't have cruel lines about his mouth. A cruel judge is a cruel man, and as a judge he does little favor to the law by his application of it. A judge who has a set rule for trying criminals--who says that every man who carries a pistol shall be fined so much; or that every thief, regardless of age or color, shall suffer to such and such degree--that judge may not be a fool, but he will have a hard time before the final judgment bar. For man is a creature of passions and repentance, and when he sins openly a judge may break him at the wheel and blast him for life, or extend the mercy that he is allowed to extend under the law, and by words of advice save a life from further sin and for happiness and good deeds. Too severe punishment belittles the majesty of the law. History for all times shows that to be true. The judges who moved as scourges never caused decrease in crime. Breaking the law is inevitable; but law breakers act from varied motives, and are men of different temperaments. Some have been tempted sorely; some have been hasty; some have been thoughtless, and have already repented; and some are hardened and deserve the deepest damnation. Such aggregation fills every court room--old men, young men, proud men, shameless men--men whose whole future lives are to be affected by the quick decision of a judge who, in his heart, does not pretend to do more than speak his character as a man.

So, as a cure for evil, the judge has a dangerous responsibility. If he deals alike with all men, he can have no knowledge of human nature, no pity, or no respect for the noble purpose of his high office. I have seen judges who looked too tenderly on all sinners. I have also seen judges in North Carolina who did not possess the quality of mercy. I have watched the works of the different judges; and I believe that cruelty in the name of the law is a crime that is unpardonable in the eyes of heaven. Common sense, an understanding of his fellow man, and a kind heart--these qualities every judge should have. But if he has them not--if he lets his merciless character as a man speak in his office of judge, he shall do evil all the days of his official life.

A Point in Theology

In the last issue of his paper, Rev. B--says:

"The Idle Comment column of the Charlotte Observer is always a very readable corner of that excellent paper. In fact, the high esteem in which that paper is held by our people generally makes its utterances on any topic exceedingly important. One having thus the ear of the public, and having the prerogative of speaking with authority, should weigh very carefully every utterance, and make sure that the cause of religious truth and faith is not made to suffer because of loose or unguarded statements. In this column in a recent issue we find the following:

"At the tent meeting last night the preacher said that on the judgment day God would laugh at the calamity of the sinner and mock at his fear. Do you think He will do that? There must be punishment. One feels that, somehow. But it isn't even human to laugh at suffering. It is inconceivable that God should be other than tender and gentle, even in His sternness.'

"Perhaps the preacher should have been more explicit, but it now stands the author of these idle comments in hand to go a step further with his cogitations and tell the reader exactly what is meant in Prov. 1:26. Perhaps if he and Brother Montgomery will get together they can give us an interpretation that will neither discredit the character of God nor help the cause of scepticism."

No, Mr. B--, the writer of the comment column will not attempt to give an interpretation of any portion of the Scriptures, and he would be sorry if he were strong enough or weak enough to say anything that would help the cause of scepticism. He believes that God does not laugh or mock at calamity; and he is not foolish enough to attempt an argument or explanation that you do not wish to provoke. It is man's privilege to believe that God's mercy is limitless; and in considering the inevitable punishment there is honor, and not discredit, to the character of God in believing that He will sorrow over human suffering. Is it wrong or sceptical to believe in the infinite tenderness and gentleness of the God of the Christians?

And no loose talk about religious matters was intended. Only a fool so talks; and any man who is not a fool must see that the Christian religion is the only basis for perfect happiness. The comment man, who shrinks from obtruding his personality into this matter, merely ventured to express a simple opinion, and if he deserves rebuke from you, Brother B--, he will receive it silently. Whatever he may be personally, his head is bowed under the admonishment of the man of God. He has learned to revere above all other persons those simple, earnest men who lovingly uphold the teachings of religion and condemn ceaselessly any deviation from the one faith. Such men the world admires and trusts to the utmost.

No; no harm, nor aught but respect and honesty was meant. With this assertion the writer would withdraw from perilous ground. In such matters he holds no further right to speech than to join the rest of mankind in despising those ghastly play-actors who occasionally desecrate a pulpit. God never created a creature of more ineffable horror and baseness than the man-thing who smirks and prates in the temple and has naught of love or fairness in his dealings with his fellow man. Here is the real dead-weight on Christianity-- the man who has conceit in his theology and is a cad at heart.

The Preacher

The world may or may not be in a state of spiritual decadence, but the time will never come when it will fail to admire and reverence the preacher who is a good man and a gentleman--not a gentleman as a snob would use the term, but a gentle, clean man who is above littleness in thought or action. Such men are the best beloved in this country; and in heathen lands--the writer has watched them there--they are the men who conquer in the name of their Master. The worst man living trusts a good preacher as implicitly as he would trust his own mother. And it is a mistaken idea that the carnal world fixes an exacting standard for a preacher. Mankind in the aggregate is not a fool, and it merely asks that a preacher shall be a gentleman, that he shall try to be good, and that he shall try to help others to be good.

Between good preachers and sinners there is never any misunderstanding. To the sinner, the preacher is the biggest man he knows, and the preacher knows this without presuming on his knowledge. The two may never get together, but the one will never give offense to the other. The old-time man of God is the model presented here. Did you ever know him to fail to win respect and liking universal?

No; when a preacher is cursed a preacher deserves cursing. Put a pin there. Everybody in this country went to Sunday-school, knows good men by intuition, and respects them naturally or as a part of a creed, and when men rise up to say that a preacher has in him the elements of a bad man he stands face to face with a truth that cannot be cried down by a whine, nor hidden under cloth that is worn as a mask. A sinner knows a bad preacher by an instinct, and has the same contempt for him that he has for any malignant, mouthing buffoon. There is no chance for misjudgment here. The bad man who is a preacher stands naked in the eyes of other men. He is far too large a blot on purity to escape unnoticed.

Good preachers neither fear nor receive the criticism that impugns character or motives. They know that their positions in a community are settled by the silent voice of that community, and there is never any dissatisfaction over the result. This statement is provoked by the fact that occasionally one hears the complaint that a minister or his church is not accorded a proper dignity or respect. That is all nonsense. Critics neither hurt nor bother churches or good preachers, and they criticise those who bring shame to a high calling because there is nothing else to do but criticise. It is quite right that this should be so.

And the narrowing eyes that scan bad preachers do not beam ill nature, though they recognize the essence of fraud and the most horrid mockery. The bad old monks were merely laughed at, and the bad preacher of these days is generally given a wide range and unlimited license. All that the world asks him to do is to refrain from doing or saying things that might cause him to be cut to shreds with a dog-whip if he happened to be unprotected by a clergyman's coat.

Humor and Pathos

A correspondent in the Observer speaks of the kinship between humor and sadness, and asks if humorists are not sad men or melancholy men. He uses sad and melancholy as synonyms. That is wrong. Sadness is a sane, tender thing. A melancholy person is morbid or fanciful, just as melancholia is one definition of insanity. But since the world was young it has been sadness and humor side by side. Both are not to be confused with other emotions. Sadness besets a soul that is tired for cause and has a dignity of its own. Humor is kind and gentle, and is mocked by many imitators. The two qualities bless each other, and sadness would be the chiefest curse if it were not accompanied by humor. The test of the question is to be applied to everyday living.

It is known that most of the greatest humorists were sad men; and yet, on the other hand, there is genuine humor in books that were written by the sunniest people. But as one lives and moves about and touches people he learns that humor is the handmaiden of sadness. Sadness is the heartache, and humor comes direct from the heart. Fun provokes a throat laugh; humor moves deeply and leaves an impression. Sometimes one is swamped in misery, and would die if it were not for the humor--brave, sweet, gentle. There is humor that would make one weep, and it is the best. And humor and tears are never very far apart. A little while ago a man died here--died in poverty, and his death marked the close of a career that had given every promise of success and happiness. He died yet young. He saw failure behind him and destitution for his children. He had to die so slowly and thoughtfully. And humor stepped in and saved him from the ghastliest punishment for the little while he had to breathe. He had a true sense of humor--grave, playful humor that allowed him to give what comfort he could to himself and those who were at his bedside. He died almost with a laugh --a good laugh. Sadness had encompassed him every second, and yet his humor was keener and dearer than it had ever been in his life. It is always so, isn't it? The sigh comes before or after the best mirth. So just in little ways the kinship is noted. Both qualities grow in the same soil. Sadness is a part of love or is caused by love; and humor is most lovable. In its essence sadness speaks the real heart of man through humor. In best sense sadness and humor are as fine, as purified and as sacred as the inner emotion of a good woman . . . and both walk with love and unselfishness.

No. 97

No. 97! And the public now has a picture in its mind. Bounding out of the North, a lean racer, trimmed for speed and endurance, the fast mail comes with the swiftness of the wind yet in titanic velocity. There were trains before, but nothing like the fast mail--this gray gleam by day and ball of fire by night. What a mad, glorious career for an unweighted, uncollared thing! Thrice she was crushed, and once so completely that when the hush came only the voice of a bird caroled above the dead. But ever out of ruin No. 97 arises, clean, beautiful, clipper-built, and leaps forth, thin-harnessed, short-coupled, and races fiercely out of the quick North down through the sleepy old South. Hands are held out to other trains and they stop; but No. 97 flies with a majestic challenge, a wild creature with one grand, resistless errand. Ghosts travel with No. 97--ay, too many poor ghosts whose wail arises in the roar that is the high scream of progress, the triumphant shout of the tragedy queen.

Slavery Books & African American History Resources
https://slaverybooks.blogspot.com

www.ingramcontent.com/pod-product-compliance
Lightning Source LLC
Chambersburg PA
CBHW081917170426
43200CB00014B/2757